A LAYMAN'S GUIDE TO THE
GREEK GODS

ALAN & MAUREEN CARTER

A LAYMAN'S GUIDE TO THE
GREEK
GODS

EFSTATHIADIS GROUP

Efstathiadis Group S.A.
Agiou Athanasiou Street,
GR - 145 65 Anixi, Attikis

ISBN 960 226 488 8

© Efstathiadis Group A.E. 1995

Printed and bound in Greece by Efstathiadis Group S.A.

To our good friend and fellow expatriot John Townsend for his invaluable assistance in the checking of the script

Our countless Greek friends who so naturally became the epitome of the ancient Greek Gods.

The authors now live in the Argolid region of the Peloponnese at Palaia Epidauros, a beautiful setting on the Eastern coast looking toward the peninsular of Methana and the islands of Aegina and Agistri.

Palaia Epidauros (Ancient Epidauros) dates back to pre-Mycenean times and was the guardian of the Sanctuary of Asclepius, which houses the world famous theatre. It was once a major city of some 80.000 inhabitants. Relatively unexcavated it has its own small theatre (circa 400 BC), temple ruins accredited to Aphrodite and Athena, Mycenean shaft graves and the sunken remains of parts of the old city.

Contents

A Guide to the Greek Gods

Introduction

When early man first emerged from his womb like cave existence and, blinking in the light, began to wonder about his surroundings, the elements and his relationship to them, we, who can look back in the light of thousands of years of development, can perhaps imagine him groping in the darkness of his incomprehension. He had to relate to his environment, find an explanation for fearful or awesome events which were beyond his control and he needed to know how he himself came to be.

From east to west, from north to south, each of these emerging races sought for their own explanations and attributed most phenomena to supernatural and powerful beings - the Gods. While each of these peoples began to deify in its own way the sun and moon, night and day, earth and water, life and death, we may be struck by many similarities between the different cults that evolved.

The Incas had the god Viracocha, the god of rain, and the god Pachacanac, the giver of life to the earth. The fertile land was in existence when Viracocha, who had neither flesh nor bones, emerged from the water to create the sun, the moon and the stars. The god Supai lived in the darkness inside the earth.

To the Egyptians, Nun was the ocean in which there lived a formless spirit, Atum, from which came Atum-Ra, the creator, the sun god from whom came all living things. Shu, the air god, on order from Ra, slipped between Geb, the earth god, and Nut, the sky god, throwing them apart and keeping Nut up high with his upraised arms.

The Old Testament of the Hebrews gives us a familiar account of creation beginning with a formless being to which we give the name God, who existed in a dark and desolate place. From God came the oceans, followed by light. Then God separated light from the darkness before creating the sky. Bringing sky and water together he formed the earth, made it fertile and then created the stars, sun and the moon.

And what of Greece? Greece with its great mountains, ice topped in winter and ablaze with flowers in the spring, arid in summer and green after the first rains of winter; Greece with its starlit night skies, dramatic sunrises - a land of vines surrounded by ever changing seas? Where the Greeks were different from previous civilisations was that they saw their Gods mainly as human forms with characteristics and personalities that are evident today in ourselves, that is, with human attributes and weaknesses. One would expect Greece to have Gods to match its landscape, cruel, majestic, beautiful, teasing, romantic, wine loving; the Gods of gods. Who were they?

There are various versions of the lineage and nature of the Greek Gods. About 800 years BC, two Greek poets, Homer and Hesiod, were writing of these deities. In Homer's epic poems we can read much about the Gods and their adventures but it is Hesiod who took the various Gods of Greece and gave them a genealogy, a family tree, in his poem 'The Theogony' and gave his explanation of Creation, beginning with Chaos.

Chaos was a dark space. Then there was Gaea, the earth, the Mother Goddess, and Eros, also without form but that which would bring together and direct the shaping of all things. From Chaos came Erebus, the darkness within the earth and Night which gave birth to Ether, the air and to Hemera, the day. Gaea produced Uranus, the starry sky, followed by the high mountains and the sterile sea. From earth and sky were born the first beings, not human yet but still Gods, in human form.

Classical Greece, the very source of much modern learning, was to emerge and grow under the strong influence of and belief in the Greek Gods. Their advice and guidance were constantly sought, the point of contact being the countless temples, shrines and monuments that were erected in their honour. The oracle, which could always be construed to fit the occasion, decided the next move on the chess board of progress and these divine messages determined the fate of many of the people.

These times produced a race of supermen and a host of geniuses, almost gods themselves, inspired by the deeds and actions of their Gods. And when that Classical era was in decline, plundered by the conquering Romans, those same Gods were adopted and revered by them to inspire their dominant period.

Greek Mythology touches on our lives in many ways. Various episodes figure in our history books, in classical writings, poems and even our fairy stories. Throughout our lives we constantly make reference to the Greek Gods and their adventures and characteristics. We say 'As strong as Hercules', 'A Herculean task', an 'Achilles' heel'. We talk about 'The Oedipus complex', 'Pandora's box', the 'Horn of Plenty' and the 'Pan pipes', These are just a few examples of sayings which we regularly use and which originate in Greek mythology.

Perhaps we should all attempt to become more familiar with the ancient Gods and, in particular, with Greek mythology which heralded the Classical Age and which is the foundation of modern learning and the cornerstone of western civilisation as we know it today. There is a thin line that separates the Gods from recorded history. It is evident yet cannot be placed.

Before the time of Homer and Hesiod, on the island of Crete, the great earth mother was worshipped by a pre-Hellenic civilisation. They also worshipped the Minotaur, the Bull god, which was housed in a labyrinth. And it is through a labyrinth of myth and legend, of agreement and disagreement, using the writings of the late Robert Graves in his talented and detailed interpretations of the Greek Myths, the work of Larousse and various other sources that we have laboured to arrive at what is, we hope, a clear and simple illustrated account, a Guide to the Greek Gods.

Throughout the text, we have attempted to record Gods or immortals in capital letters and mortals in normal print, although we acknowledge that many grey areas exist as to actual status.

Although we have listed the Gods as far as possible in order of appearance, it is as well to remember that time did not exist as we know it for the immortals. These ageless Gods lived outside time and continued to exist alongside each other, the first with the last, unless confined to the deepest Underworld or placed in the Heavens as stars.

THE
OLYMPIAN CREATION

Chart 1

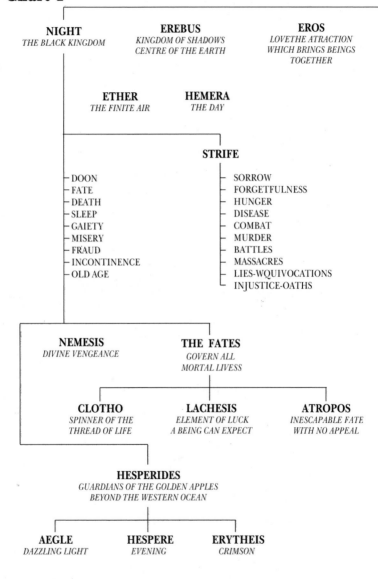

NIGHT
THE BLACK KINGDOM

EREBUS
KINGDOM OF SHADOWS
CENTRE OF THE EARTH

EROS
LOVETHE ATRACTION
WHICH BRINGS BEINGS
TOGETHER

ETHER
THE FINITE AIR

HEMERA
THE DAY

STRIFE

- DOON
- FATE
- DEATH
- SLEEP
- GAIETY
- MISERY
- FRAUD
- INCONTINENCE
- OLD AGE

- SORROW
- FORGETFULNESS
- HUNGER
- DISEASE
- COMBAT
- MURDER
- BATTLES
- MASSACRES
- LIES-WQUIVOCATIONS
- INJUSTICE-OATHS

NEMESIS
DIVINE VENGEANCE

THE FATES
GOVERN ALL
MORTAL LIVESS

CLOTHO
SPINNER OF THE
THREAD OF LIFE

LACHESIS
ELEMENT OF LUCK
A BEING CAN EXPECT

ATROPOS
INESCAPABLE FATE
WITH NO APPEAL

HESPERIDES
GUARDIANS OF THE GOLDEN APPLES
BEYOND THE WESTERN OCEAN

AEGLE
DAZZLING LIGHT

HESPERE
EVENING

ERYTHEIS
CRIMSON

CREATION OF THE UNIVERSE

(Chart No. 1 will aid the comprehension of the difficult geneaology, and is strictly linked to the text.)

And in the beginning there was CHAOS, not a God but a cosmic principle, an idea in the mind of man, vast, existing without shape or substance and representing dark, infinite space.

Chaos, a dark space

An apt description comes from Norse mythology where, in the Elder Edda, a wise woman, speaking of the Scandinavian concept of the beginning of time, says:

Of old there was nothing.
Nor sand, nor sea, nor cool waves.
No earth, no heaven above.
Only the yawning chasm.
The sun knew not her dwelling
Nor the moon her realm.
The stars had not their places.

And out of CHAOS came EROS, another insubstantial concept, bringing harmony to CHAOS. EROS, a love which softened hearts and provided the atrraction which brought beings together, permitted life to begin. This EROS later became the personification of Love.

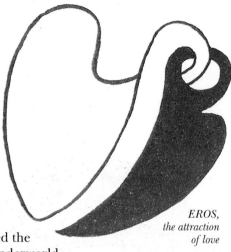

*EROS,
the attraction
of love*

Also out of CHAOS came EREBUS, the Kingdom of Shadows and TARTARUS the Kingdom of Hell, which together formed the two divisions of the underworld, a mysterious region of desolation, approached by caves and underground rivers. TARTARUS was the deeper of the two kingdoms which were situated at the centre of the earth, and was the place of punishment for some of the Gods or their enemies. EREBUS was to become the reception centre for the dead.

*EREBUS,
the shadow
at the centre
of the earth*

Black NIGHT came from CHAOS, united with EREBUS and now we have light in the

darkness, for together they created
ETHER, the finite air and HEMERA, the
day.

EREBUS &
NIGHT create
ETHER &
HEMERA

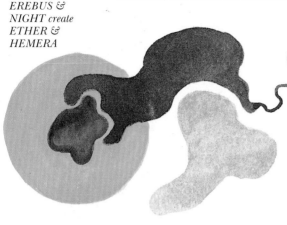

EREBUS &
NIGHT create
ETHER &
HEMERA

GAEA,
Mother Earth

THE CREATION OF
THE GODS

Finally out of CHAOS
came GAEA, the
universal Mother
Goddess from whom all
things issued. She was known
to the Romans as TELLUS
and she symbolised the earth
whose soil nourished all living
things. She created the Universe
and bore the first race of Gods.

She was the forerunner of the
human race and presided over
marriages and the sick.

She was the keeper of the Delphic oracle
until she passed the authority of its wisdom
over to APOLLO, although some say that
THEMIS was an intermediary.
GAEA was the original cult figure to the
inhabitants of Greece and she was
commonly represented as a gigantic deep
breasted woman, the oldest of the divinities.

GAEA began her creation of the Universe
by forming URANUS, the sky with its
crown of stars and she made him equal to
her, such that he entirely covered his
mother earth.

GAEA then created the
high mountains and PONTUS, the sterile
sea with its harmonious waves.

URANUS

*PONTUS the
sterile sea*

At this point the universe was complete. So far GAEA has only created inanimate matter and now came the creation of Gods in the shape of humans who would symbolise the tumultuous forces of nature.

Earth (GAEA) and sky (URANUS), who were to become known as the grandparents of the world, combined to produce the first race of Gods, the TITANS and TITANESSES, some of whom we know more about than others.

There were six TITANS in the order of appearance:

OCEANUS, the great river that surrounds the earth. The ancient Greeks thought that there was a huge river which encircled the universe. Not to be confused with PONTUS, OCEANUS came into contact with the sea without combining with it.

OCEANUS

COEUS, the intelligent. HYPERION, the dweller on high and father of the sun, moon and dawn, later to be dethroned by APOLLO.

CRIUS, whose name meant the male sheep or Ram.

IAPETUS, who was called the hurrier.

CRONUS, Father Time, the crow. This was the youngest TITAN who would eventually continue the work begun by GAEA.

IEPETUS

There were six TITANESSES in order of appearance:

THEIA, the divine one, her name means 'Shining'.
RHEA, mother of the great ruling gods of Olympus.
MNEMOSYNE, mother of the Muses and the personification of Memory.
PHOEBE, the bright moon.
TETHYS, the disposer who would determine the course of events.
THEMIS, the Goddess of Law and the keeper of Order.

THE TITANS and the TITANESSES were regarded as the ancestors of man and the origin of magic and the arts.
GAEA and URANUS then produced the CYCLOPES known as the Storm Genii. They were a race of one eyed giants

The CYCLOP STEROPES

who were reputed to be skilled craftsmen and were said to have built Athens and the walls of Tiryns. They were the main

assistants of HEPHAESTUS, the smith God, and were particularly associated with the manufacture of ZEUS' thunderbolts. They were:
BRONTES, the thunder.
STEROPES, the lightning.
ARGES, the thunderbolt

Finally from the union of **GAEA** with URANUS came the **HECATONCHEIRES**, also known as the **CENTIMANES**. They were monsters called:
COTTUS, the furious.
BRIAREUS, the strong.

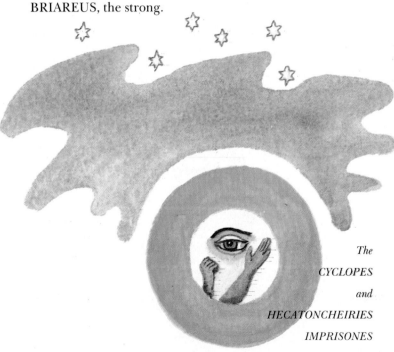

The CYCLOPES and HECATONCHEIRIES IMPRISONES

GYGES, the big limbed.

The three HECATONCHEIRES, meaning the hundred hands, were monsters from whose shoulders grew a hundred arms and from these limbs rose fifty heads.

URANUS was so horrified with his dreadful offspring in the form of the CYCLOPES and the HECATONCHEIRES that he imprisoned them in the depths of the earth, TARTARUS.

GAEA, however, devastated at the loss of her children, became angry and she planned the mutilation of her partner URANUS. She explained her intended revenge to her sons and daughters, the TITANS and TITANESSES, but they were revolted by the idea, except for CRONUS who agreed to assist his mother with her terrible scheme.

GAEA produced shining steel from her bosom and from this she fashioned a sharp sickle which she gave to CRONUS. When URANUS came to GAEA at night, CRONUS, who had been placed in hiding, waited until URANUS was asleep, then attacked him and with the sharp sickle he severed his manhood.

The bloody sickle

CRONUS cast the genitals into the sea where they floated and became a white foam from which was born a young Goddess called APHRODITE. She was carried on the waves by ZEPHYRUS, the west wind, riding on a scallop shell, first to Kythera and then onward to Paphos on

A GIANT

Cyprus where she is especially revered to this day. Here she was cared for by the HORAE, or SEASONS, daughters of ZEUS and THEMIS. Wherever she stood, grass and flowers grew and her constant companions were doves and sparrows.

APHRODITE was the Goddess of Love who wore a magic girdle around her waist which made her beautiful and irresistibly desirable.

Black blood poured from the terrible wounds of URANUS onto the earth and immediately gave birth to:
The redoubtable ERINYES, to be known to the Romans as The FURIES. They lived in EREBUS and were the personification of conscience. They would avenge the sins of mortals, such crimes as of children against parents, hosts against guests and treachery, and they pursued their victims without mercy. They were known as 'The Kindly Ones' and 'The Holy Ones' to please them as it was not considered sensible to use their real names. They were represented as winged women with snakes about them. Their names were:

ALECTO
MEGAERA
TISIPHONE

The monstrous GIANTS or GIGANTES were also born out of the wounds of URANUS. They were partly human, of huge size, with serpents for feet.

The Ash Tree NYMPHS or MELIAE, carrying spears of ashwood, were the last to come from the black blood of URANUS. Nymphs were female personifications, young and beautiful, fond of music and dancing, long lived but not immortal.

A NYMPH

They possessed gifts such as prophecy,
were usually gentle but occasionally
formidable. They resembled fairies.
URANUS having been reduced to
impotence, CRONUS took over the work of
creation at this point, leaving the
CYCLOPES and the HECATONCHEIRES

imprisoned in TARTARUS.

Under the rule of CRONUS, NIGHT created:
DOOM or MOROS.

FATE or BLACK KER. A great and phenomenal force, not a God but having more power than the Gods, she was never to be underestimated as to spurn her would bring down the anger of NEMESIS, about whom we will read soon.

NIGHT creates SLEEP

DEATH, THANATOS, and SLEEP, HYPNOS. DEATH and SLEEP lived in the underworld from where men received their dreams. Authentic dreams passed through a gateway of horn while false dreams went through one of ivory.MOMUS, the personification of criticism,and MISERY or OIZUS. NIGHT also created the three HESPERIDES who guarded the golden apples beyond the western ocean where they lived in a wonderful garden and were the personification of clouds which gleamed gold in the setting sun.

They were known as HESPERE, AEGLE and ERYTHEIS.

Then NIGHT created the three FATES or MOIRAE, known as:

CLOTHO, who represents the thread of life and spins it on her loom.

LACHESIS, who represents the element of luck a person has the right to expect, and ATROPOS, the inescapable fate against which there was no appeal.

The FATES were to

CLOTHO the thread of life

Fate apportions good & evil

apportion good and evil to all future mortals. They would govern the whole of a person's

life - his inescapable destiny - and their will would be executed by the KERES.

NEMESIS maintains the human equilibrium

NIGHT further created: NEMESIS, the divine vengeance that would pursue and punish any mortal who offended or displeased the Gods either by transgressing against the moral law and thus incurring their wrath or by attaining too much happiness or riches and thus exciting their jealousy.

NIGHT
creates Old Age

NEMESIS
was to
maintain the
inexorable
equilibrium of the human condition.

Finally NIGHT created FRAUD
INCONTINENCE
OLD AGE STRIFE or ERIS.
STRIFE continued the creation producing:

SORROW
FORGETFULNESS
HUNGER
DISEASE
COMBAT
BATTLES
MASSACRES
LIES AND EQUIVOCATION INJUSTICE
and OATHS.

GAEA coupled with PONTUS to produce

COMBAT

NEREUS, the truthful, a benevolent and ancient sea god, capable of prophecy, who could change his appearance at will.

THAMUS, the monstrous or wonderful.

PHORCUS, the intrepid, wise son of the sea and earth, who had a female equivalent in the form of PHORCIS the Goddess or sow.

CETO, with the pretty cheeks, and EURYBIA, with the heart of steel whose name means wide strength.

PHORCIS the sow

NEREUS paired with DORIS (the Bountiful), who was the nymph daughter of the ocean, and together they produced fifty daughters known as the NEREIDS who were cousins of the HARPIES and the PHORCIDS.

The NEREIDS were a college of fifty Moon Priestesses in the form of mermaids whose magic rites ensured good fishing. They were beautiful, these nymphs of the sea and two of them were destined to become famous in Mythology. They were THETIS and GALATEA and they lived in the depths of the sea in a palace.

The three HARPIES were loathsome winged female creatures, otherwise known as Snatchers, who lived underground in caverns. They were the fair haired and swift winged daughters of THAUMUS and the ocean nymph ELECTRA who were also the parents of:

IRIS, the Goddess of the rainbow, a messenger of the greater Gods, especially of HERA. She is depicted with wings, wearing winged boots and carrying a staff and is shown standing next to HERA on the frieze of the Parthenon. Perhaps she is a messenger of the Gods because the rainbow seems to touch both the sky and the earth.

The PHORCIDS were the children of PHORCYS and CETO and comprised:
LADON, (the Embracer), who was a dragon capable of human speech and who also guarded the golden apples with the HESPERIDES.

ECHIDNE, (the She Viper), half woman, half serpent, who

was a cave dweller. She ate humans without bothering to cook them first.

The three GORGONS who were grotesque sisters with snakes in their hair and around their waists. Anyone who looked at them was turned to stone. Only Medusa was mortal and she was to be killed by the Hero, Perseus, after she had slept with POSEIDON and carried his child. From her blood would spring PEGASUS, the winged horse.
The GORGONS were named STHEINO (the strong), EURYALE (wide roaming) and MEDUSA (the cunning one) and were known as the grim ones.

Lastly the three GRAEAE who protected their sisters, the GORGONS, and were the personification of old age.

The GRAEAE

They were fair faced and swan like but with grey hair from birth and one only eye and

and one tooth between the three of them.
They were called ENYO (warlike),
PEMPHREDO (wasp) and DEINO
(terrible).

ECHIDNE, or the She Viper, was to join
with the monster, TYPHON, the scourge of
mankind (you will learn more of him later),
to produce a dreadful brood, namely:

The HYDRA

CERBERUS the three headed
hound of hell (the demon
of the pit). who guarded
the way in to HADES
and who conducted souls to
the underworld; the HYDRA,
a multi headed
water serpent
which
dwelled at Lerna in the
marshes. One of its heads
was immortal and if any of
the others was cut off, two
grew in its place;
the CHIMAERA, a fire
breathing goat with a
lion's head and a
serpent's body,
representing the three
seasons, the tripartite
year or Spring,
Summer and
Winter.

From its name comes our word 'chimera' meaning a fanciful notion;and finally ORTHRUS, the two headed watch dog hound who guarded the cattle of Geryon, a three bodied monster who lived on the western island of Erythia and was the king of Tartessus in Spain. He was reputedly the strongest man alive.

ORTHRUS was to combine with his mother ECHIDNE to further produce both the SPHINX, the throttler who had a woman's head, a serpent's tail and an eagle's wings. This female strangled those who could not solve her riddle: 'What walks on four legs at dawn, on two at noon and on three in the evening?' It was to be answered eventually by OEDIPUS.

And the NEMEAN LION, an enormous beast with a pelt proof against iron, bronze and stone. No weapon could wound it.

We will meet all this dreadful brood later in significant episodes of the adventures of the Greek Gods and Heroes.

Readers, the scene is set, the universe has been created, the initial Gods have taken up their places, good and evil lie in wait, emotions are present. All the elements will play their tricks and man's path will be strewn with endeavour, courage, temptation and faith.

Let the story continue:

THE OFFSPRING GODS
OF THE TITANS

Chart 2
OLYMPIC CREATION - "THE GOLDEN AGE"

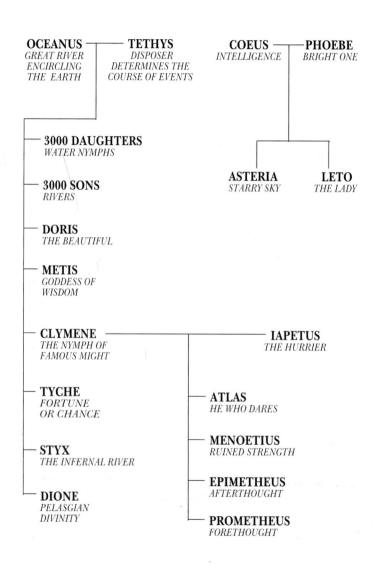

OCEANUS — **TETHYS**
GREAT RIVER *DISPOSER*
ENCIRCLING *DETERMINES THE*
THE EARTH *COURSE OF EVENTS*

COEUS — **PHOEBE**
INTELLIGENCE *BRIGHT ONE*

3000 DAUGHTERS
WATER NYMPHS

3000 SONS
RIVERS

DORIS
THE BEAUTIFUL

METIS
GODDESS OF
WISDOM

ASTERIA
STARRY SKY

LETO
THE LADY

CLYMENE —————————————— **IAPETUS**
THE NYMPH OF *THE HURRIER*
FAMOUS MIGHT

TYCHE
FORTUNE
OR CHANCE

ATLAS
HE WHO DARES

MENOETIUS
RUINED STRENGTH

STYX
THE INFERNAL RIVER

EPIMETHEUS
AFTERTHOUGHT

DIONE
PELASGIAN
DIVINITY

PROMETHEUS
FORETHOUGHT

RHEA
*MOTHER OF THE GREAT
RULING-GODS OF OLYMPUS*

CRONUS
*THE CROW.
FATHER TIME*

PHILYRA
*NYMPH DAUGHTER
OF OCEANUS*

CHIRON
*CENTAUR
HALF HORSE
HALFMAN*

HESTIA
*GODDESS OF THE
DOMESTIC HEARTH*

DEMETER
THE BARLEY MOTHER

HERA
THE PROTECTRESS

HADEΣ
GOD OF THE UNDERWORLD

POSEIDON
GOD OF THE SEA

ZEUS
KING OF THE GODS

THEMIS
*THE KEEPE
OF ORDEF*

THE HORAE
THE SEASONS

EUNOMIA
WISE LEGISLATION

DIKE
JUSTICE

EIRENE
PEACE

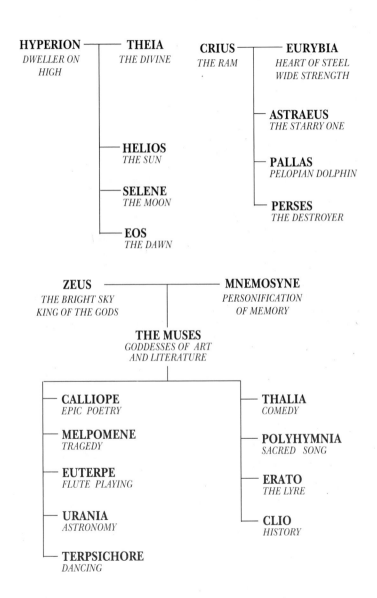

HYPERION
DWELLER ON HIGH

THEIA
THE DIVINE

HELIOS
THE SUN

SELENE
THE MOON

EOS
THE DAWN

CRIUS
THE RAM

EURYBIA
HEART OF STEEL
WIDE STRENGTH

ASTRAEUS
THE STARRY ONE

PALLAS
PELOPIAN DOLPHIN

PERSES
THE DESTROYER

ZEUS
THE BRIGHT SKY
KING OF THE GODS

MNEMOSYNE
PERSONIFICATION
OF MEMORY

THE MUSES
GODDESSES OF ART
AND LITERATURE

CALLIOPE
EPIC POETRY

MELPOMENE
TRAGEDY

EUTERPE
FLUTE PLAYING

URANIA
ASTRONOMY

TERPSICHORE
DANCING

THALIA
COMEDY

POLYHYMNIA
SACRED SONG

ERATO
THE LYRE

CLIO
HISTORY

This period is known as the Golden Age under the rule of CRONUS who took as his incestuous partner RHEA, his sister.

However, it had been prophesied by GAEA and URANUS that CRONUS would be dethroned by one of his offspring. In order to negate the prophecy, CRONUS swallowed each of his children as they were born.

The first born was
HESTIA, the Goddess of the domestic hearth. She was a virgin who was worshipped by every family. After birth a child was carried around the hearth before it could be embraced into the family. Every city had a hearth dedicated to HESTIA, situated in a public place and where the fire was never allowed to go out.
The second born was DEMETER, the

*CRONUS swallows
his children*

barley mother and the Goddess of the threshing floor and agriculture in general.. Harvest time was her festival but the rites of worship were mysterious and secret and known only to the initiated.

The third born was HERA, the Queen of Heaven, who orginally had power over all life but eventually became the Goddess of marriage. The favoured females of her unfaithful husband, ZEUS, were to feel the force of her anger. She was born on the island of Samos, spending her childhood on Euboea.

The fourth born was HADES and, as with the FURIES, it was considered unsafe to use his name but wiser to favour him with a more pleasant title, PLUTO. He ruled the underworld

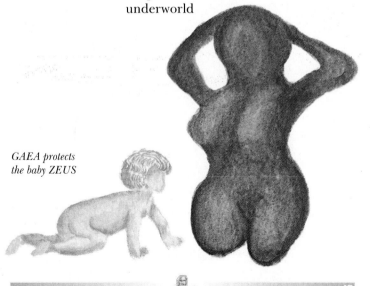

GAEA protects the baby ZEUS

which consisted of both EREBUS and TARTARUS and was named after him. The fifth born was POSEIDON, he who provides drink from the wooded mountain and guards the sea. He had an underwater palace where he kept the horses which drew his golden chariot across the sea, thus calming the waters which he could also command to rage and storm.

Each of these, CRONUS swallowed but RHEA was determined that this should not continue. So when her sixth child was born, she sent the child to GAEA for protection and substituted within the child's shawl a large stone. Without glancing inside the wrapping, CRONUS duly swallowed what he

Water Nymph

imagined to be the sixth born.

This sixth child was ZEUS, the bright sky, who was destined to become the God of Gods. You will hear much more of him.

The Olympian creation continued with the marriage of

OCEANUS to TETHYS, his TITANESS sister. They were to produce 3,000 sons, the rivers of the world and 3,000 daughters, the water nymphs.

They also produced:

A daughter, METIS, the Goddess of Wisdom who knew more than anyone. She counselled the young ZEUS and became his first wife.

TYCHE

TYCHE, the Goddess of fortune and chance, that unfathomable ingredient of life which can bring either good or evil. Her name means 'that which happens', and she could give plenty to some and take everything from others.

STYX was a river spirit residing in the infernal river of hate, the Styx, the main river of the underworld which it encircled before entering. When the TITANS warred against ZEUS, STYX was there to help him and, as a reward, she was regarded as unassailable by the Gods.

DIONE

CLYMENE

DIONE, the Pelasgian Divinity. The Pelasgians, or sea people, were reputed to be the original race in Greece prior to the Hellenes and the Achaeans. Her name is the feminine of ZEUS and means 'Divine Queen'. She was the Goddess of the oak tree.

And the nymph CLYMENE or famous might.

It was CLYMENE who was to couple with her Titan uncle IAPETUS to produce:

ATLAS

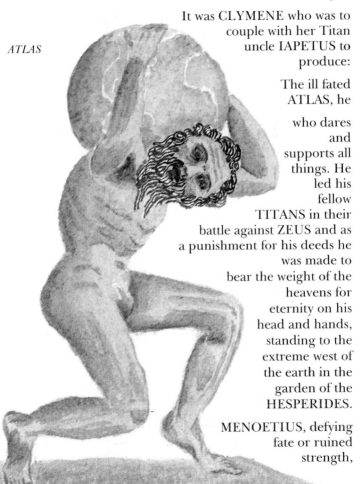

The ill fated ATLAS, he

who dares and supports all things. He led his fellow TITANS in their battle against ZEUS and as a punishment for his deeds he was made to bear the weight of the heavens for eternity on his head and hands, standing to the extreme west of the earth in the garden of the HESPERIDES.

MENOETIUS, defying fate or ruined strength,

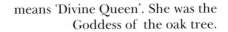

associated with the Oak cult of which he was the sacred king. The members of the cult believed the mistletoe to be the oak tree's genitals and practised the ritual of mistletoe castration.

MENOETIUS joined ATLAS in the war of the TITANS and for this he was killed by a thunderbolt from ZEUS and banished to TARTARUS.

The oak cult

And finally PROMETHEUS and his brother EPIMETHEUS. PROMETHEUS, who possessed the gift of forethought, was an important God as some say that it was he who took clay and fashioned it into the first man. During CRONUS' golden age, men and Gods lived and ate together in harmony but ZEUS, when he came to rule, changed this in his desire to reign supreme. This probably upset PROMETHEUS who was very much on the side of man and, at a meeting to decide which pieces of sacrificial victims were due to the Gods, PROMETHEUS played a trick. It was his job to divide a great ox. He put the best meat on one side covered by the hide and laid out the bones, covering them with succulent pieces of fat, on the other side.

ZEUS had first choice and, picking the glossy fat, fell into a rage on discovering only bones beneath it. He reacted by withholding fire from man but PROMETHEUS stole it, possibly by lighting a brand from the sun, and carried it back to the mortals, amongst whom he helped instigate the arts and trade.

ZEUS retaliated by having a beautiful woman made out of clay by his skilful son, HEPHAESTUS. This first female was named PANDORA and ZEUS sent her as a gift, accompanied by a great urn, not to PROMETHEUS but to his brother EPIMETHEUS, whose chief characteristic was unfortunate afterthought. Armed with his gift of forethought, PROMETHEUS warned his brother not to accept the God's present but EPIMETHEUS ignored the warning and took her, being dazzled by her beauty and failing to see the danger in the urn she carried. PANDORA opened her urn from which escaped evil and suffering to spread all over the earth, leaving only hope at the bottom.

EPIMETHEUS

ZEUS had not finished with
PROMETHEUS, who kept to himself a
secret concerning ZEUS' love affair with
THETIS, who was the fairest of the
Nereids. The God had him chained to a
rock on Mount Caucasus and sent an eagle
to feed upon his liver which was, of course,
immortal, so this torture continued for
many years, the liver growing back as fast as
it was devoured, until PROMETHEUS was
released, some say by HERACLES and
others say that he finally revealed the secret
to ZEUS.

PROMETHEUS

A union was
created between
HYPERION and
THEIA and they
would produce:

HELIOS, who
personified the sun
and was
worshipped from
ancient times. He
rode across the sky
each day in a
golden chariot
pulled by
winged horses, coming
from the east and
rising into the
heavens, reaching
the highest point at
midday, his golden
helmet flashing

and sparkling. He rode on to the west and descended into the land of the Hesperides from where he sailed the Ocean all night with his family in a golden cup until he reached the east once more.

The light of HELIOS shone on all things and nothing was secret from him, thus he was able to uncover a love affair of APHRODITE. She took her revenge by filling HELIOS with love for a mortal, Leucothea, daughter of a certain king, Orchamos. Leucothea's sister, Clytie, was jealous and revealed the liaison to Orchamus who, in his anger, had Leucothea buried alive. HELIOS tried unsuccessfully to restore her to life with his warmth, eventually turning her into a shrub. Clytie, still passionately in love with HELIOS and knowing that her feelings would never be returned, died of despair, her body becoming one with the soil, taking root in the earth. Her head grew into a bright flower, always facing her beloved HELIOS. She had become the fragrant, purple heliotrope.

Whilst he was revered, the worship of HELIOS did not become a regular cult, except on the island of Rhodes, because he did not frequent the earth, as did the Olympian Gods. Rhodes was the island he chose for his own after he had been erroneously omitted from the distribution of land by ZEUS. There, HELIOS married the nymph, Rhode, and had three sons, namely Lindus, Ialysus and Kamirus, after whom the three ancient cities of Rhodes were named. An annual festival took place in his honour, called the Halieia, which included athletic contests.

SELENE, the moon Goddess, renowned for her beauty. Each evening, rising from the Ocean, she began a journey into the sky as her brother HELIOS finished his own. She fell in love with a mortal, ENDYMION, who asked ZEUS to give him eternal youth and immortality. ZEUS gave him his wish but only on condition that he slept forever. SELENE came each night to see her sleeping lover and the light of her beauty shone on all sleeping mortals.

EOS, the lovely Goddess of the dawn. She rose early from the Ocean as the moonlight of SELENE faded, to bring the first flicker of incandescent daylight into the heavens. Dressed in yellow, she would tip dew from an urn onto the earth, sometimes astride the winged horse, PEGASUS, and other times riding in a purple chariot.

Pairing with the TITAN, ASTREUS, EOS became the mother of the four winds but also made an enemy of APHRODITE when ARES fell in love with her. The jealous APHRODITE, in retaliation, ensured that EOS loved certain mortals, the first being Tithonus. EOS asked ZEUS to give her lover immortality but forgot to also request eternal youth for him. Consequently Tithonus grew old over the years until he was eventually turned into a cicada by the compassionate Gods.

HELIOS

By Tithonus, EOS bore a son, Memnon, who became a warrior king of Ethiopia.

He was to be killed by the Hero, Achilles, and the tears which EOS shed daily for her beloved son formed the dew which filled her urn.

The North Wind

COEUS coupled with PHOEBE to produce:

LETO, the lady destined to be the mother of APOLLO and ARTEMIS. Hesiod said of her that she was 'Gentle to men and to the deathless Gods'. Unusual for a Titaness, she had a cult following. A legend has it that while escaping from the clutches of HERA when attempting to give birth to ZEUS' children, APOLLO and ARTEMIS, she took on the form of a shewolf. Thus disguised, she journeyed to the eventual birthplace, the island of Delos, the journey taking twelve days, As a result there are only twelve days in a year when she-wolves can give birth.

COEUS and PHOEBE also produced ASTERIA, the starry sky who was destined to become the island of Delos.

CRIUS, the revered God of the Peloponnese, whose name means male sheep or ram, coupled with EURYBIA and they were to produce:

ASTRAEUS, the starry one who with EOS was to produce BOREAS, EURUS, NOTUS and ZEPHYRUS, the North, East,

NIKE

South and West winds, also PHOSPHORUS and some say all the other stars of Heaven.

PALLAS, an allegory of the Pelopian dolphin sacred to the Moon Goddess who was to couple with STYX and father:

PERSES
the Destroyer

ZEIUS, rivalry
CRATUS, strength
BIA, force and
NIKE, victory.

These four were honoured by ZEUS for their part in defeating the TITANS. NIKE in particular became the symbol of decisive victory, ruling over all competition, including military, athletic and musical.Later to be known to the Romans as VICTORIA, she was particularly revered in Olympia, the famous site where athletes gathered to contest their skills and where the famous statue of winged NIKE is now on display.

Finally they produced the destructive PERSES.

The Titaness MNEMOSYNE joined with her nephew ZEUS and produced:

The nine MUSES being:

CALLIOPE, epic poetry
MELPOMENE, tragedy,
EUTERPE, flute playing
URANIA, astronomy
TERPSICHORE, dancing
THALIA, comedy
POLYHYMNIA, sacred song
ERATO, the lyre
CLIO, history

Finally, at this stage, CRONUS courted the Oceanid, PHILYRA and when discovered by his wife, RHEA, in the act of seduction, he changed himself and PHILYRA into horses. It was from this union that CHIRON, the Centaur, half man and half horse, was born. PHILYRA was so horrified at producing the Centaur that she begged the Gods to change her own shape. Her wish was granted and she became the Linden tree.

URANIA

THE RISE OF ZEUS

Chart 3

MNEMOSYNE
PERSONIFICATION OF
MEMORY

THE MUSES
GODDESES OF THE ARTS AND LITERATURE

THEMIS
KEEPER OF
ORDER

HORAE	**EUNOMIA**	**DIKE**	**EIRENE**
THE SEASONS	*WISE LEGISLATION*	*JUSTICE*	*PEACE*

DEMETER
THE BARLEY MOTHER

PERSEPHONE
BRINGER OF DESTRUCTION

HERA
PROTECTRESS

ARES	**HEPHAESTUS**	**HEBE**	**ILITHIA**
THE WAR GOD	*SMITH GOD*	*YOUTH*	*THE MIDWIFE*

METIS
GODDESS OF
WISDOM

ATHENA
QUEEN OF HEAVEN

LETO
THE LADY

APOLLO	**ARTEMIS**
DESTROYER	*THE HUNTRESS PATRONESS OF CHILDBIRTH*

EURYNOME
DAUGHTER OF
THE OCEAN

AGLAIA	**EUPHROSYNE**	**THALIA**
SPLENDOR	*MIRTH*	*GOOD CHEER*

EUROPA
PHOENICIAN
PRINCESS

MINOS	**RHADAMANTHYS**	**SARPEDON**
CREATURE OF THE MOON	*WAND DIVINER*	*OR THE WOODEN ARK*

MAIA
ARCADIAN NYMPH
OF THE FAIR TRESSES

HERMES
MESSENGER OF ZEUS

LEDA
THE LADY WIFE
OF TYNDAREUS

POLLUX	**HELEN**
OF THE DIOSCURI WITH CASTOR	*OF TROY FAME*

ZEUS
THE BRIGHT SKY KING OF THE GODS

SEMELE
DAUGHTER OF CADMUS
KING OF THEBES
DIONYSUS
GOD OF WINE

ANTIOPE
DAUGHTER
OF NYCTEUS
AMPHION
HARPER
ZETHUS
FOUNDER OF THEBES

ALCMENE
WOMAN OF MIGHT
HERACLES
PERSONIFICATION OF STRENGTH

AEGINA
NYMPH
AEACUS
BEWAILER

NIOBE
THE SNOW
MORTAL WOMAN
ARGOS
FOUND OF ARGOS

PLUTO
OCEANID
TANTALUS
MOST WRETCHED

DANAE
DAUGHTER
OF ACRISIUS
PERSEUS
THE DESTROYER

PROTOGENIA
DAUGHTER
OF DEUCALION
OPUNS
FOUNDER OF OPUNTIAN LOCRIS

THALIA
THE MUSE
COMEDY
PALICI
TWINS DIOSCURI OF SICILY

MERA
NYMPH
LOCRI
ANCESTOR OF THE LOCRIANS

IO
DAUGHTER OF THE
RIVERGOD INACHUS

EPAPHUS
THE TOUCHING

HESIONE
DANAID

ORCHOMENUS
STRENGTH OF BATTLE

OLENUS
FOUNDER OF OLENUS
IN ACHAIA

ANAXITHEA
DANAID

DIA
WIFE OF IXION

PIRITHOUS
KING OF THE LAPITHAE

ELARA
DAUGHTER OF
ORCHOMENUS

TITYUS
THE GIANT

TAYGETE
DAUGHTER OF ATLAS

LACEDAEMON
FOUNDER OF SPARTA

CALLISTO
THE FAIREST NYMPH

ARCAS
THE BEAR ANCESTOR
OF THE ARCADIANS

CARME

BRITOMARTIS
CRETAN GODDESS

CRONUS was not aware of the existence of ZEUS, who had been taken to Crete by GAEA and placed in the care of the Nymphs ADRASTEIA and IDA, the daughters of King Melisseus (honeyman) of Crete.

ZEUS was placed in a golden cradle and he played with a ball made from golden hoops. The noise of his crying was hidden from his father CRONUS by the constant noise of the CURATES, Cretan priests later to become the Sacred CURATES, protectors of ZEUS.

The golden ball of ZEUS

ZEUS grew up on Mount Ida nursed by a remarkable she-goat named AMALTHEIA who had marvellous horns which contained nectar and ambrosia. Her appearance frightened even the immortals. ZEUS later was to show his gratitude to her by placing her amongst the constellations as the star, Capella. He broke off one of her horns which he filled with luscious fruits and presented it to the nymphs. This had the remarkable property of automatically refilling itself, thus replenishing any food or drink they desired. This horn of plenty or cornucopia is a term much used today. Finally, from her hide, ZEUS fashioned an

The horn of plenty

upper
garment or
'aegis', which
would be proof against any weapon for the
wearer.

The prophecy which had predicted that
CRONUS would be dispossessed by one of
his offspring was to come true. ZEUS was
committed to overthrow and punish his
father.

With the aid of METIS, a draught was
given to CRONUS that made him vomit up
the five children and the stone which he
had swallowed.

These five brothers and sisters of ZEUS
were known as the New Gods and the stone
which had been disgorged was placed in
Pytho at the foot of Mount Parnassus as a
symbol of his famous victory over his father.

CRONUS was defeated by ZEUS, driven to
the very depths of the universe and there

enchained. Some say that earthquakes ever since are the strains of CRONUS attempting to break free from his bondage.

The TITANS, apart from OCEANUS, were jealous of these new Gods and wished to re-conquer the kingdom which they had lost. A terrible struggle, to last ten years, was the result, and ZEUS released the CYCLOPES and HECATONCHEIRES from captivity in order to recruit their assistance. Together, they crushed the TITANS, bound them with chains and imprisoned them in the bowels of the earth amongst extreme darkness and foul smells.

CRONUS
tries to break free

You will remember that from the blood of URANUS had come the GIGANTES or giants with serpents for feet, (See chart 1) and they were the next to challenge the authority of ZEUS. Clad in their shining armour and armed with ice from Mount Athos, they attacked ZEUS and his Gods, piling Mount Ossa onto Mount Pelion in order to reach Olympus. They were to be repelled by the incredible skill of the Gods and of APOLLO, HEPHAESTUS, ARES and POSEIDON in particular.

However, the oracle had prophesied that, in order to succeed against the GIGANTES, it had to be a mortal who would seal their fate. Such a mortal was the Hero, HERACLES, (whose exploits you can read about in our stories of the Greek Heroes), and in punishment ZEUS ordered that they be buried under various volcanoes where they lay fuming for ever more.

Finally, ZEUS maintained his supremacy with the defeat of TYPHOEUS, who was a terrifying monster produced by GAEA from her union with TARTARUS.

TYPHOEUS, whose hands worked ceaselessly and whose feet were never still, had one hundred dragon heads spitting fire. Snakes emerged from his thighs, his body was covered in feathers and thick bristles grew from his

TYPHOEUS

head and face. Taller than the tallest mountain, he was a truly formidable foe. At the sight of this horrible monster, all the Gods fled in terror, disguising themselves as animals. Only ATHENE stood her ground and persuaded ZEUS to return and fight. In the ensuing battle, TYPHOEUS imprisoned ZEUS in a cave, having first removed the sinews from his wrists and ankles, rendering the God powerless. The cave was guarded by DELPHYNE, a serpent-tailed fellow monster.

It was HERMES and PAN who came to the rescue of ZEUS. PAN, with a terrifying cry, frightened the monster DELPHYNE, and during this distraction, HERMES retrieved the sinews and replaced them in ZEUS' limbs.

Battle recommenced, and now ZEUS was aided by the three FATES, who weakened TYPHOEUS by feeding him poisoned fruits. ZEUS' thunderbolts

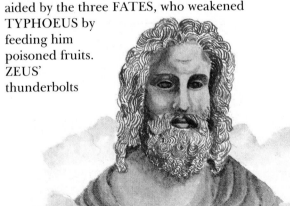

ZEUS

finally vanquished the monster and he was buried under Mount Etna, in Sicily, where his fire still smoulders.

And so, finally, peace and harmony were restored and praise was heaped on ZEUS, the God who had triumphed against the forces or evil. ZEUS was now the indisputable master of Gods and men. He was destined to be revered from the highest mountains and the most holy places in Greece.

ZEUS was ZEUS! He saw everything and knew everything. Indeed whichever way history has twisted or interpreted its roots, ZEUS would appear to be the epitome of some people's understanding of God. He was moral, divine, omnipotent, and dispensed both good and evil. Today, when we are trying to explain the awful tragedies that befall different areas and races of the Earth, or illnesses, afflictions and early or senseless death, perhaps we should remember that even ZEUS was controlled by the FATES who together with NEMESIS would determine the length and quality of the life of mortal man.

Like mortals, the Gods experienced human passions and emotions. They dispensed favours and punished enmity. However no Greek Gods could be heroic. They were all both immortal and invincible. They could never feel the glow of courage nor could they experience danger. Their differences from mortals were, firstly, that their blood was replaced by ichor containing healing and eternal youth properties and, secondly, they had the power of metamorphosis which meant that they could change themselves at will into any animal or inanimate object they desired.

Set against the prolific prowess of ZEUS, the latterday Casanova and Bluebeard would sink into insignificance.

His supremacy as God of Gods and his powers of metamorphosis provided access to any union or liaison he desired and he was to produce a family, some of whose names have become very familiar to us.

EIRENE,
Goddess of Peace

ZEUS obtained absolute wisdom when he married METIS, the Goddess of Wisdom and then swallowed both her and her unborn child because he had learned through an oracle from GAEA that a boy offspring by METIS would be more knowledgeable and more powerful than he and would eventually depose him in the same way that ZEUS had deposed CRONUS and CRONUS had deposed URANUS. Later, ZEUS suffered a terrible headache and was demented by the pain. His son, HERMES, divined the cause of the affliction and he persuaded another of his sons, HEPHAESTUS, to open the skull with an axe. From the wound sprang a daughter, ATHENE, with a mighty shout. She was fully clothed in armour with a helmet, shield and spear.

His next wife was THEMIS, his aunt, who represented the law. So it not unnaturally follows that this union should produce THE HORAE, (seasons) whose names were: EUNOMIA (wise legislation), DIKE (justice) and EIRENE (peace).

Having discarded THEMIS as a wife, he was to retain her as an adviser when she took her place on Olympus. His next wife was his aunt, MNEMOSYNE, with whom he laid for nine nights. From this marriage came the nine MUSES.

He was to marry EURYNOME, an oceanid, from whom came the GRACES or CHARITIES, attendants on the greater Gods.

ZEUS then married HERA, his older sister. Not to awaken her suspicions, he came to her in the form of a cuckoo. The cuckoo was looking cold from the frost and HERA warmed it against her breast. It was then that ZEUS reversed the metamorphosis and, regaining his own shape, made love to HERA after undertaking to marry her. He kept his promise and, after a three hundred year honeymoon in Samos (remember the Gods are ageless and timeless), the union produced ILYTHIA (the Goddess of child birth), the gracious HEBE, (the Goddess of youth), disagreeable ARES, (the God of war) and the skilful HEPHAESTUS (the smith God). Enamoured by his older sister, DEMETER, ZEUS was to change himself into a bull in order to rape her, the offspring being PERSEPHONE or KORE, who was destined to become the wife of his brother HADES.

LETO surrendered to his charm and, despite the wrath of HERA, managed to bear APOLLO and ARTEMIS. The story goes thus:

After LETO had been made pregnant by ZEUS, she searched desperately for a place to give birth to the child in safety and to escape from the relentless pursuit of the jealous HERA and the monster PYTHON. Most places, fearing the wrath of HERA, turned her away. However, LETO's sister, ASTERIA, had been transformed into a floating island, Ortygia, and it was here that LETO was made welcome. To make things even more difficult for LETO, HERA had vowed that the birth could only occur in a place where the light of the sun never penetrated, and here POSEIDON came to LETO's aid. He made the waves form a dome over Ortygia and anchored the island firmly to the sea bed with four columns.

ASTERIA the floating island

In a rage, HERA refused to allow the Goddess of childbirth, ILITHYIA, to attend

LETO who endured terrible suffering for nine days as a result. Eventually IRIS was sent to Olympus to bring ILITHYIA to help and the rainbow twins were born, namely APOLLO and ARTEMIS. After the birth, the island Ortygia became Delos, meaning the brilliant, and it is famous for a decree which still holds good today, that no one shall be born or die there.

APOLLO was nourished, not on his mother's milk, but on a mixture of ambrosia and nectar, ambrosia being the food which gave the Gods their immortality. Nurtured in this way, APOLLO quickly developed a manly physique and set out on an urgent undertaking to seek and destroy the female dragon monster known as PYTHON, which HERA had unsuccessfully sent to kill LETO prior to APOLLO's birth. Armed with arrows forged for him by HEPHAESTUS, APOLLO located PYTHON in the gorge of Parnassus and slew the monster whose death throes marked the spot known as PYTHO, which means to rot, and which was later to become the world renowned site of Delphi.

ZEUS as an eagle

ZEUS then turned his

attentions to MAIA, one of the seven Pleiades, daughters of ATLAS and PLEIONE. She lived in the depths of a dark cavern in Arcadia. and from this union came HERMES.

ZEUS then pursued another of the Pleiades, called TAYGETE. The girl, in desperation, called to ARTEMIS for help, and was turned into a hind as a disguise. In appreciation, TAYGETE presented ARTEMIS with a hind with golden horns and which will figure in later stories of the Heroes. However, ZEUS did eventually ravish TAYGETE and a son called LACEDAEMON was born. In her shame, TAYGETE hung herself on the summit of Mount Amyclaeus, known today as Mount Taygete.

AEGINA was a nymph who was loved by ZEUS. In order to take her from her father, the river God ASOPUS, he assumed the form of an eagle and took her to the island of Oenopia. There she gave birth to AEACUS.

ASOPUS came looking for his abducted daughter and, to save AEGINA from the paternal wrath, ZEUS turned her into the island which now lies in the Saronic Gulf.

ANTIOPE was another nymph who was loved by ZEUS who surprised her in her sleep disguised as a Satyr. She fled to Sicyon and her father NYCTEUS committed suicide at her loss. There she married EPOPEUS but he was killed by LYCUS, the brother of NYCTEUS, in order to avenge his death. ANTIOPE gave birth to twins named AMPHION and ZETHUS who were to become major figures in Theban legend as rulers of Thebes. Together they built the walls of the city, AMPHION playing the harp and conjuring the building blocks into place with his music. ZETHUS was to marry the nymph THEBE from whence the name of Thebes was derived.

CALLISTO, the nymph daughter of LYCAON, was a companion of the huntress ARTEMIS. ZEUS took on the form of ARTEMIS in order to get close to CALLISTO. Later, when CALLISTO was bathing, it enraged ARTEMIS to see that she was with child. To shield

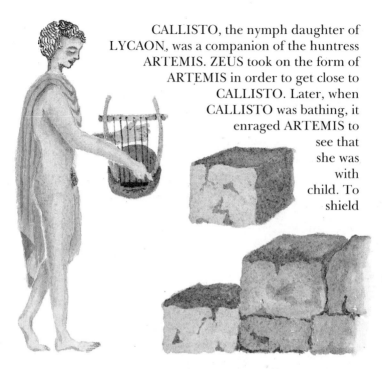

AMPHION

CALLISTO, ZEUS changed her into a bear but she was killed by the arrows of ARTEMIS as she was giving birth to ARCAS, the bear that was to be the ancestor of the Arcadians.

CALLISTO was elevated to the heavens to become the constellation which we call the Great Bear.

MERA, the daughter of PRAETUS, was also killed by her protectress ARTEMIS for having consorted with ZEUS. Before dying she gave birth to LOCRI, the ancestor of the Locrians.

Niobe was the first mortal woman that ZEUS loved and she was to bear Argos, the founder of that ancient city.

Niobe's aunt was Io, who resided in the Heraeum near Argos, where she was a priestess to HERA. ZEUS took the form of a cloud in order to seduce her but his wife HERA was suspicious. And so he changed Io into a white heifer. But HERA was not deceived and asked for the heifer as a present. She put it in the care of ARGUS PANOPTES, a giant who had one hundred

HERA's peacock

eyes, always with fifty open. ZEUS enlisted the aid of HERMES to free Io and he succeeded by charming the giant to fall asleep with the quality of his flute playing and then cut off his head.

HERA was to honour the giant in perpetuity by endowing his eyes to the tail of her favourite bird, the peacock. As for Io, she was plagued by a gadfly sent to sting and torture the heifer. Io fled to avoid the fly. She crossed the now named Ionian sea to Egypt where ZEUS restored her to human form and she bore him the child Epaphus, the bearer of touch.

Acrisius, who ruled Argos, had one daughter named Danae. It had been prophesied that Danae would produce a son who would kill Acrisius and, to protect himself, he imprisoned his daughter underground in a bronze chamber together with her nurse. In order to

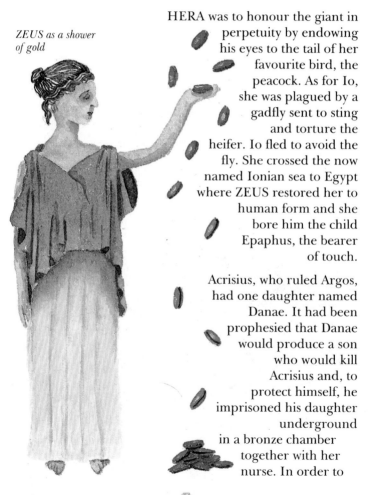

ZEUS as a shower of gold

get to her, ZEUS took the form of a shower of gold and this resulted in the birth of the Hero, Perseus. Acrisius further protected himself by locking Danae and her baby in a chest which was thrown into the sea. However, in a storm, the chest was washed up on the island of Seriphus where a fisherman Dictys found it in his nets. As we shall see later in episodes of the Heroes, Perseus would fulfill the prophecy.

The next lover of ZEUS was Semele, the daughter of Cadmus. When HERA discovered this

ZEUS as a bull

affair, she went to Semele in disguise and said she should ask her lover to show her his real self. Semele insisted that ZEUS should do this for her, unaware that she would be consumed in flames at the sight of the great God in his chariot. ZEUS gathered the unborn baby and protected it in his own thigh until ready for birth. The baby was DIONYSUS, about whom you will read soon.

Europa was the daughter of the king of Phoenicia and she was raped by ZEUS in the form of a bull. While playing near the lakeside, she saw this gentle, friendly bull who responded to her strokes, but she was suddenly captured and conveyed across the sea to Gortyna in Crete to give birth to Minos, Rhadamanthys and Sarpedon. All three became the adopted sons of the king of Crete, Asterius, who Europa married.

The next target of ZEUS was the wife of Tyndareus, called Leda. When Leda was bathing in the pool, she saw coming towards her a beautiful white swan who was ZEUS in disguise. She was ravished by the God, also receiving the attentions, that same night, of her husband. Two eggs were produced, one containing POLLUX and HELEN from the seed of ZEUS and the other containing Castor and Clytemnestra from the seed of Tyndareus. HELEN and Clytemnestra were destined to be linked tragically with Troy, the subject of Homer's Iliad. Castor and POLLUX, known as the inseparable twins, the DIOSCURI, were famous for their athletic prowess. They were honoured by ZEUS, who placed them in the heavens as the GEMINI.

ZEUS set his heart on Alcmene, the wife of the Theban ruler Amphitryon, and he seduced her by taking on the guise of her husband when he was away. Amphitryon returned that same day and was as mystified at her lack of enthusiasm for him as she was mystified at his powers of

recovery. From this day's activity, Alcmene produced twin
sons, HERACLES, son of ZEUS and Iphicles, son of Amphitryon.

ZEUS was insatiable in his love affairs. The Oceanid PLUTO was to produce the wretched TANTALUS.

TANTALUS was invited to live with the Gods and share their food, thus eating ambrosia, which gave him immortality. TANTALUS, however, repaid the generosity of the Gods by stealing food and giving it to mortals, for which deed he was punished severely. He was destined to stand in water up to

TANTALUS

his chin while over his head grew luscious fruits. When he tried to drink, the water receded and when he tried to eat, the wind blew away the fruit. So he was condemned to hunger and thirst forever, to be 'tantalized', as we would say today, by having whatever he wanted so near to him and yet unattainable.

By ZEUS, the Danaid Anaxithea gave birth to Olenus and the Danaid Hesione gave birth to Orchomenus, by whose daughter, Elara, ZEUS fathered a giant, Tityus. The birth of this giant took place underground where Elara had been hidden to escape the jealousy and wrath of HERA.

ZEUS carried off Protogenia from her husband, Locre, and she bore him a son, Opuns.

Then there was THALIA, the MUSE of comedy, who with ZEUS was to produce the twins known as the Palici, the Dioscuri of Sicily.

ZEUS then took on the form of a horse in order to seduce Dia, the wife of Ixion, and this union produced Pirithous, who was a king of the Lapithae and will feature prominently in the stories of the Heroes.

Finally we will record his affair with CARME in Crete, the offspring being BRITOMARTIS, the Cretan Goddess.

Despite his infidelities, ZEUS too could have his jealous moments and he was to punish Ixion, another king of the Lapithae, for desiring his wife, HERA. He trapped Ixion by creating a cloud in the shape of HERA. When Ixion embraced the cloud in mistake for her, he had to confess his desire and the jealous ZEUS had him bound to a flaming wheel that would traverse the sky in perpetuity.

It would not be difficult to select from various historical writings even more of ZEUS' liaisons but we have to stop

somewhere and certainly we have covered
the major offspring of which we will hear
much more.

IXION

THE HIERARCHY

THE MAJOR OLYMPIAN GODS AND GODDESSES

ZEUS
(ROMAN JUPITER)
*KING OF THE GODS GOD
OF THE SKY SON OF
CRONUS AND RHEA*

ATHENE
(ROMAN MINERVA)
*THE WARRIOR GODDESS
PROTECTRESS OF CITIES
DAUGHTER OF ZEUS AND METIS*

HERA
(ROMAN JUNO)
*QUEEN OF THE SKY
SISTER AND WIFE OF ZEUS*

ARTEMIS
(ROMAN DIANA)
*GODDESS OF CHILDBIRTH
DAUGHTER OF ZEUS AND LETO
SISTER OF APOLLO*

APOLLO
(ROMAN APOLLO)
*GOD OF DIVINATION AND
PROPHECY SON OF ZEUS AND
LETOBROTHER OF ARTEMIS*

ARES
(ROMAN MARS)
*THE GOD OF WAR
SON OF ZEUS AND HERA
BROTHER OF HEPHAESTUS*

HERMES
(ROMAN MERCURY)
*THE MESSENGER OF ZEUS
GOD OF COMMERCE
AND ATHLETICS
SON OF ZEUS AND MAIA*

APHRODITE
(ROMAN VENUS)
*GODDESS OF LOVE
FEMININE BEAUTY
DAUGHTER OF URANUS*

HEPHAESTUS
(ROMAN VULCAN)
*THE ARTISAN GOD
THE DIVINE BLACKSMITH
SON OF ZEUS AND HERA
BROTHER OF ARES*

HESTIA
(ROMAN VESTA)
*GODDESS OF THE DOMESTIC
HEARTH A FIRE DIVINITY
SISTER OF ZEUS*

POSEIDON
(ROMAN NEPTUNE)
*GOD OF THE SEA
THE EARTH SHAKER
BROTHER OF ZEUS AND HADES*

HADES
(ROMAN PLUTO)
*GOD OF THE UNDERWORLD.
BROTHER OF ZEUS AND POSEIDON
NOTE: - HE CHOSE NOT TO TAKE UP
HIS PLACE ON OLYMPUS*

DEMETER
(ROMAN CERES)
*GODDESS OF THE CULTIVATED SOIL
THE BARLEY MOTHER SISTER
OF ZEUS*

Chart 5

THE HIERARCHY (A)

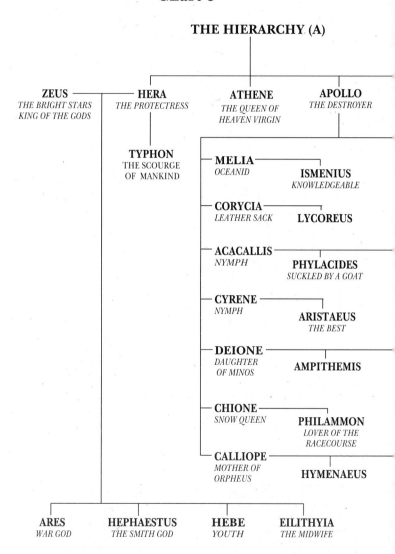

ZEUS
THE BRIGHT STARS
KING OF THE GODS

HERA
THE PROTECTRESS

ATHENE
THE QUEEN OF
HEAVEN VIRGIN

APOLLO
THE DESTROYER

TYPHON
THE SCOURGE
OF MANKIND

MELIA
OCEANID

ISMENIUS
KNOWLEDGEABLE

CORYCIA
LEATHER SACK

LYCOREUS

ACACALLIS
NYMPH

PHYLACIDES
SUCKLED BY A GOAT

CYRENE
NYMPH

ARISTAEUS
THE BEST

DEIONE
DAUGHTER
OF MINOS

AMPITHEMIS

CHIONE
SNOW QUEEN

PHILAMMON
LOVER OF THE
RACECOURSE

CALLIOPE
MOTHER OF
ORPHEUS

HYMENAEUS

ARES
WAR GOD

HEPHAESTUS
THE SMITH GOD

HEBE
YOUTH

EILITHYIA
THE MIDWIFE

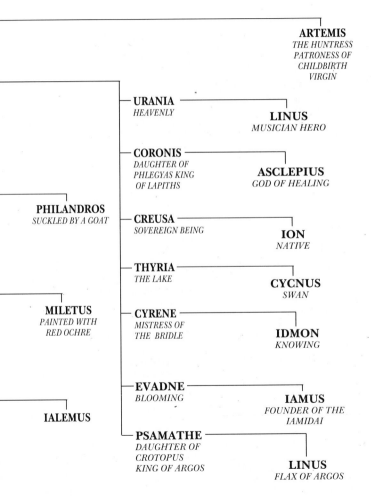

ARTEMIS
THE HUNTRESS
PATRONESS OF
CHILDBIRTH
VIRGIN

URANIA
HEAVENLY

LINUS
MUSICIAN HERO

CORONIS
DAUGHTER OF
PHLEGYAS KING
OF LAPITHS

ASCLEPIUS
GOD OF HEALING

PHILANDROS
SUCKLED BY A GOAT

CREUSA
SOVEREIGN BEING

ION
NATIVE

THYRIA
THE LAKE

CYCNUS
SWAN

MILETUS
PAINTED WITH
RED OCHRE

CYRENE
MISTRESS OF
THE BRIDLE

IDMON
KNOWING

EVADNE
BLOOMING

IAMUS
FOUNDER OF THE
IAMIDAI

IALEMUS

PSAMATHE
DAUGHTER OF
CROTOPUS
KING OF ARGOS

LINUS
FLAX OF ARGOS

Chart 6

THE HIERARCHY (B)

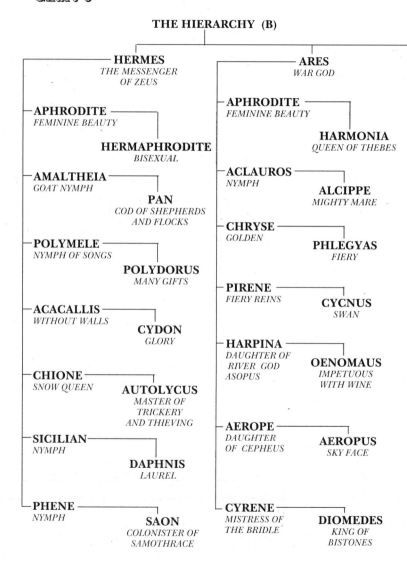

HERMES
THE MESSENGER OF ZEUS

ARES
WAR GOD

APHRODITE
FEMININE BEAUTY

HERMAPHRODITE
BISEXUAL

APHRODITE
FEMININE BEAUTY

HARMONIA
QUEEN OF THEBES

AMALTHEIA
GOAT NYMPH

PAN
COD OF SHEPHERDS AND FLOCKS

ACLAUROS
NYMPH

ALCIPPE
MIGHTY MARE

POLYMELE
NYMPH OF SONGS

POLYDORUS
MANY GIFTS

CHRYSE
GOLDEN

PHLEGYAS
FIERY

ACACALLIS
WITHOUT WALLS

CYDON
GLORY

PIRENE
FIERY REINS

CYCNUS
SWAN

CHIONE
SNOW QUEEN

AUTOLYCUS
MASTER OF TRICKERY AND THIEVING

HARPINA
DAUGHTER OF RIVER GOD ASOPUS

OENOMAUS
IMPETUOUS WITH WINE

SICILIAN
NYMPH

DAPHNIS
LAUREL

AEROPE
DAUGHTER OF CEPHEUS

AEROPUS
SKY FACE

PHENE
NYMPH

SAON
COLONISTER OF SAMOTHRACE

CYRENE
MISTRESS OF THE BRIDLE

DIOMEDES
KING OF BISTONES

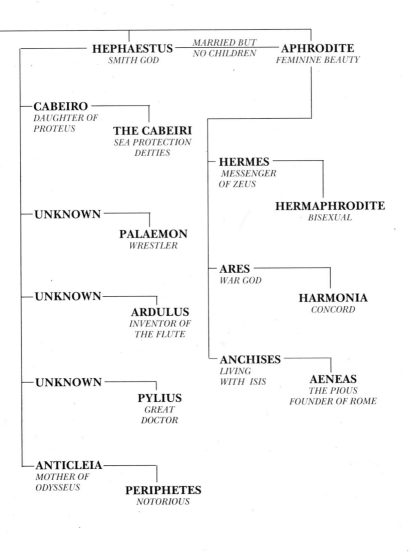

HEPHAESTUS —— *MARRIED BUT NO CHILDREN* —— **APHRODITE**
SMITH GOD *FEMININE BEAUTY*

CABEIRO
DAUGHTER OF PROTEUS

THE CABEIRI
SEA PROTECTION DEITIES

HERMES
MESSENGER OF ZEUS

HERMAPHRODITE
BISEXUAL

UNKNOWN

PALAEMON
WRESTLER

ARES
WAR GOD

HARMONIA
CONCORD

UNKNOWN

ARDULUS
INVENTOR OF THE FLUTE

ANCHISES
LIVING WITH ISIS

AENEAS
THE PIOUS FOUNDER OF ROME

UNKNOWN

PYLIUS
GREAT DOCTOR

ANTICLEIA
MOTHER OF ODYSSEUS

PERIPHETES
NOTORIOUS

Chart 7

POSEIDON
GOD OF THE SEA

AMPHITRITE
FEMININE SEA

TRITON
THIRD DAY

RHODE
ROSY

BENTHESICYME
WAVE OF THE DEEP

CHIONE
SNOW QUEEN

THEOPHANE
*APPEARANCE OF
THE GODDESS*

DEMETER
*THE BARLEY
MOTHER*

ARION
WILD HORSE

ALOPE
*SLY AS
A VIXEN*

GAEA
*UNIVERSAL
MOTHER*

ANTAEUS
GIANT

MEDUSA
CUNNING

CHRYSAOR
GOLDEN FALCHION

PEGASUS
OF THE WELLS

AMYMONE
BLAMELESS

ANIPPE
*QUEENLY
MARE*

CELAENO
HARPY

EURYPYLUS
WIDE GATE

LYCUS
WOLF

TYRO
NYMPH

PELIAS
BLACK-BLUE

NELE US
RUTHLESS

MELIA
ASH TREE

IPHIMEDEIA
*STRENGTHENER
OF GENITALS*

EPHIALTES
*TWINS THE
ALOEDAE*

OTUS

THOOSA
NYMPH

POLYPHEMUS
CYCLOP

CALYCE
ROSEBUD

THE HIERARCHY (C)

HESTIA
THE GODDESS OF THE DOMESTIC HEARTH VIRGIN

DEMETER
THE BARLEY MOTHER

ZEUS
THE BRIGHT SKY

PERSEPHONE
BRINGER OF DESTRUCTION

EUMOLPUS
GOOD MELODY

POSEIDON
GOD OF THE SEA

ARION
WILD HORSE

RAM WITH THE GOLDEN FLEECE

IASION
HEALING NATIVE

PLUTUS
WEALTH

HIPPOTHOUS
IMPETUOUS STALLION

EUROPA
PHOENICIAN PRINCESS

EUPHEMUS
RELIGIOUS SILENCE

PITANE

EVADNE
BLOOMING

NAUPLIAS
NAVIGATOR

EURYTE
WIDE ACTIVITY

HALLRHOTHIUS
ROARING SEA

BUSIRUS
KING OF EGYPT

PIRENE
HER TEARS BECAME THE PIRENE FOUNTAIN IN CORINTH

2 SONS WHO DIED MISERABLY

MOLIONE
QUEEN OF THE WARRIORS

MOLIONIDS
TWINS

AMYCUS
LOUDLY BELLOWING

DAUGHTER OF AMPHICTYON

CERCYON
BOAR'S TAIL

CYCNUS
SWAN

ALCYONE
QUEEN WHO WARDS OFF STORMS

AETHUSA

HYRIEUS
OF THE BEEHIVES

HYPERENOR
OVERBEARING

The main dwelling place of the Gods was Olympus, the mountain chain in northern Thessaly which rises to just under 3,000 metres. This mountain range has a curvature that resembles an amphitheatre, the upper tiers being outcrops which are sometimes draped with cloud. Here were the golden thrones of ZEUS and HERA along with the seats of the other major Gods.

Mount Olympus

It is at this stage that lots had been drawn between the three sons of the defeated CRONUS.
ZEUS, whom the Romans were later to rename JUPITER, was to become the God of the Heavens. POSEIDON, whom the Romans were to call NEPTUNE, was to become the God of the Sea and HADES, renamed PLUTO by the Romans, was to be

the God of the Underworld. HADES did not take a seat on Olympus but remained in his subterranean kingdom from where he influenced the earth's crops. It is said that he possessed a special helmet which could make him invisible.

ZEUS was gifted with the armament of a Thunderbolt in order to control troublesome events and to exert his authority over whoever had the audacity to challenge his will.

ZEUS made the laws, controlled the heavens and pronounced the oracles.

His special oracle was Dodona in Epirus, where his wishes were interpreted from the rustling of the oak leaves.

His bird was the majestic eagle, which he used to fetch the beautiful youth, Ganymede, to Olympus as attendant to the Gods.

His tree was the sturdy oak and his breastplate was the awesome aegis.

There came a time when the other Olympian Gods banded together to attempt his overthrow by binding him to his couch when he slept, having first hidden his thunderbolt. The coup was to fail because THEMIS recruited BRIAREUS, the HECATONCHEIRE, to untie ZEUS with his hundred hands.

ZEUS resumed control and punished HERA, POSEIDON and APOLLO as an example to the others.

He hung HERA from the sky by golden bracelets and fastened an anvil to each foot. Her cries were awful and she was not released until all had sworn never to rebel again.

HECATONCEIRE

As for POSEIDON and APOLLO, they were punished by being subject to manual labour in the building of the city walls of Troy whose ruler was King Laomedon.

ZEUS was in control!We can now discuss the seniority and particular characteristics of the Olympian Gods.
Assembled on Olympus, the new order of Gods originated their own hierarchy and laws.

First came the twelve great Gods and Goddesses. Under ZEUS came HERA, ATHENE, APOLLO, ARTEMIS, HERMES, ARES, HEPHAESTUS, APHRODITE, POSEIDON, HESTIA and DEMETER.
Next in line came the Lesser Gods, THEMIS, METIS, DIONYSUS,PAN,HEBE, ILYTHIA, IRIS and ASCLEPIUS.

Serving them, and of lesser stature, came the HORAE, MOIRAE, NEMESIS, GRACES, and the MUSES.

HERA

Next to ZEUS came HERA, to be called JUNO by the Romans, who was the queen of heaven and the sister and wife of ZEUS. She presided over all aspects of women. She was the goddess of marriage and maternity. She depicted the ideal wife. Her image is of severe beauty crowned with a 'polos' or high crown of cylindrical shape. She wears a long tunic and her symbols are:-

The cuckoo (by which she was seduced in the metamorphosis of ZEUS).

The pomegranate (conjugal love and fruitfulness).

The peacock (whose plumage represents the heavenly stars decorated by the eyes of her faithful servant ARGUS).

The chief centre of her following was Argos with other important centres at Mycenae, Olympia, Sparta, Attica, Boeotia, Euboea, Crete and Samos. Near Argos, the Heraeum housed a gold and ivory statue of the Goddess while the largest of temples dedicated to her is thought to have been that on the island of Samos, her birthplace.

Her marriage to ZEUS must surely have eventually led to the modern saying 'Hell hath no fury like a woman scorned.'

We have already seen that, with ZEUS, they produced:-

ILYTHIA, the Goddess of childbirth.
HEBE, the Goddess of youth.
ARES, the God of war, and
HEPHAESTUS, the skilful Smith God.

On her marriage to ZEUS, HERA became the most important Goddess of Olympus, where she took her place seated on a golden throne. Of the many gifts brought to the wedding by the other Gods, one of the most impressive was a tree that grew golden apples. This present came from GAEA and was the tree that was guarded by the HESPERIDES on the western edge of the world.

Not without good cause, HERA was to become jealous of the many mistresses of ZEUS. They were constantly quarrelling and she tried many ways to humiliate and embarass him in retaliation for his unfaithfulness. She, however, was always faithful to him, avoiding would-be lovers. She made certain that she was always attractive to her husband, often annointing her body with such sweetly scented oils that, as they filled the world with their perfumes, ZEUS would remark,

Never has love for goddess or mortal woman so flooded my senses and filled my heart.'

HERA could also be spiteful and cruel to those who rivalled her in beauty, inflicting disease or madness on those who slighted her and, when ANTIGONE boasted of having lovelier hair than HERA, the jealous Goddess turned it into snakes.

The vindictiveness of HERA reached a peak when PARIS of Troy was asked to award a golden apple marked 'To the fairest' to whichever Goddess was most worthy of the prize. APHRODITE, HERA and ATHENE were the three finalists in the competition and PARIS gave the apple to APHRODITE. HERA satisified her thirst for revenge by taking the side of the Greeks in the war against Troy that followed and was not to be content until the whole of the Trojan race was destroyed.

HERA's fidelity to ZEUS was exemplary.
His unfaithfulness is legendary.

HERA implored the imprisoned TITANS
to help her bear, unaided, a child who
would be of equal strength to ZEUS. Her
wishes were granted and she gave birth to
the terrible TYPHON, the scourge of
mankind. TYPHON is not to be confused
with that other monster, TYPHOEUS,
which was the offspring of GAEA and
TARTARUS.

HERA

ATHENE

The third in line was ATHENE, also known as PALLAS ATHENA, the daughter of ZEUS and METIS the Goddess of wisdom. The Romans would re-name her MINERVA. She was to become the favourite daughter of ZEUS, thus often arousing the jealousy of the other Gods, and was venerated all over Greece in many ways.

Also known as the Warrior Goddess, her ultimate aim was to secure peace. She acted as a mediator in many instances of combat and exemplified prudent intelligence.

She was the protectress of cities and the guardian of Acropolises, many temples being raised in her honour, the most famous of these being the world renowned Parthenon on the Acropolis of Athens. The Parthenon (the name means 'Temple of the Maiden') was dedicated to ATHENE PARTHENOS, the maiden. On the site of the Parthenon, but preceeding it, had been a colossal statue of ATHENE PROMACHOS, 'the Champion', and the golden point of her spear, it was said, could be seen from the sea. There was also a temple there to ATHENE NIKE or Victory ATHENE.

In her own city of Athens she was the Goddess of Reason and presided over the arts and literature.
Her heart resisted love affairs and she was to remain chaste. Any intrusion on her modesty would be severely punished as the following story shows:
She was bathing one day with her friend, the nymph Chariclo, when she was seen, quite by chance, by Tiresias. ATHENE immediately punished him by striking him blind. Chariclo pleaded for mercy which ATHENE only partly gave, although she did not restore his sight, she gave him the power to foretell the future. Alfred Lord Tennyson

used this story when he wrote of Tiresias:

*'Henceforth be blind, for thou has seen too much
And speak the truth that no man may believe.'*

The qualities of ATHENE were numerous. She taught the art of

ATHENE

taming horses, was reputed to have invented the potter's wheel and made the first vases. She gave women the arts of weaving cloth and of embroidery and one woman named Arachne became so accomplished in the art of weaving that she challenged ATHENE to a contest in the handling of both the spindle and the needle. Indeed Arachne's work was perfect. ATHENE was unable to accept her defeat and unfairly punished her competitor. Arachne was turned into a spider, condemned eternally to spin, drawing the thread from her own body in order to construct her web.

ATHENE is normally represented as a stern beauty clothed in armour, carrying a spear and a shield embossed with the Gorgon's head. Her head is helmeted and her emblem was the owl.

APOLLO

ATHENE was followed by APOLLO, the son of ZEUS and
LETO. He retained his own name when he was later
adopted by the Romans. Whilst APOLLO means destroyer,
he was a solar God who ripened the fruits of the earth. The
first crops at Delos and Delphi were consecrated to him. His
epithets gave to him golden locks, fair complexion and
brilliant intellect. He was the God of Prophecy and was
given the Delphic oracle rights by GAEA, although you will
remember that it was possibly under the control of
THEMIS for a period. Known as a Healing God, he drove
away illness.

The bow, quiver, shepherd's crook and lyre are associated
with him.
The swan, vulture, hawk, cock, crow, cicada, wolf and
serpent were sacred to him.
He favoured the olive, tamarisk, palm and laurel trees.
He is normally naked and is depicted as a strong young
man of great beauty. He had a high forehead, thick long
hair and was beardless.

When depicted as a musician, for he was also the God of
music, he is shown wearing a long robe. The lyre, invented
by the infant HERMES, was given to APOLLO by the child,
as you will read later, in exchange for a herd of cattle.

Many sanctuaries honoured APOLLO, including Tegyra
and Thebes, but the most important is at Delphi, famous
for the power of the oracle which was delivered from a
sacred tripod called the Seat of Manto, by the chief
preistess, or Pythia, whose faculty devoted themselves to the
cult of APOLLO.

He was often in the company of the MUSES to whom the
now renowned Castalia fountain was sacred, the waters

giving inspiration to their artistic works. The MUSES honoured APOLLO and were guardians of the Delphic Oracle.

If ATHENE was the favourite daughter of ZEUS then APOLLO was his most loved son.

APOLLO was particularly respected on Olympus by the other Gods and ZEUS always welcomed him with nectar served in a golden cup.

As a bowman his arrows were infallible. He slew the giants, EPHIALTES and OTUS, when they sought to abduct HERA and his sister ARTEMIS. He also slew the giant Tityus when he made advances towards his mother LETO. In fact he showed his formidable strength on many occasions. There was the battle with Phorbas, a man of immense strength who had earned himself a sinister reputation for attacking and killing pilgrims on their way to Delphi. APOLLO dispatched Phorbas in a mighty fist fight.

Then there was a famous incident when APOLLO confronted the great HERACLES who, in his disappointment with the Delphic Oracle, had stolen the sacred tripod on which the priestess sat to deliver the divine messages. APOLLO gave chase and they were about to exchange blows when ZEUS intervened. He commanded HERACLES to return the tripod and persuaded the pair to make up their differences. Despite his youthful good looks, his strength and his considerable talents, APOLLO failed to enjoy a lasting relationship with a female. He had many amorous liaisons with some notable failures.

The beautiful nymph Daphne fled from his advances. She implored GAEA to help her and on the point of being ravished by APOLLO, she was transformed into a laurel tree which became a sacred emblem to him. Today our generic name for laurel is 'daphne'.

The mortal woman, Castalia, refused his attentions to the extent of killing herself, drowning in the Delphi fountain which took her name.

Probably the most famous son of APOLLO was ASCLEPIUS who was to become the God of healing. ASCLEPIUS was the result of a tragic affair whereby Coronis, his mother, had conceived by APOLLO but prior to the birth she married the Arcadian, Ischys.

APOLLO

Apollo was informed of the marriage by a crow which he had left to watch over Coronis. At that time, crows were white birds, but in his rage at the news APOLLO turned the crow and all crows from then on, black. He put Coronis and Ischys to death. Their bodies were put on a funeral pyre and APOLLO snatched the unborn baby from Coronis before the fire consumed the dead couple.

The father of Coronis, Philegyas, king of the Lapiths, attacked Delphi and burned the temple of Apollo when he learned of his daughter's fate, but he too was overcome by the God who threw him into Tartarus where he was tortured.

ARTEMIS

The fifth in line was ARTEMIS, twin sister of APOLLO. Later the Romans were to call her DIANA. She was the daughter of ZEUS and LETO and although a virgin, she was, together with ILITHYIA, the Goddess of childbirth and a bringer of fertility to man and beast. She was especially revered in the Peloponnese as the generator of the fruitfulness of trees. Bears, boars, wolves, goats and the smaller wild beasts and birds are particularly associated with her. At Ephesus she was worshipped as a Goddess of fertility and was depicted as being multi-breasted. Greece generally knew her as the Goddess of the hunt and of forests and her symbol was a bear.

Like her brother APOLLO, she bore a bow and arrows and was sometimes known as APPOLLOUSA, the destructress. When occasioned, she could strike down mortals with her arrows and cause disease among their herds or flocks. Her main centres of worship were Arcadia, Sparta, Athens, Aegina, Olympia and, of course, Delos, the island of her birth. ARTEMIS is normally depicted as a young, slim woman of austere beauty, wearing a short, tunic like dress and laced leather footwear. Carrying a bow and arrows, she is often accompanied by a dog or a stag.

The sympolic bear

She was born a day before her twin brother, APOLLO and in the early stages was often in his company. She went with him on his exploits against the serpent PYTHON.

Later she chose Arcadia as her favourite dwelling place and enjoyed the thrills of the chase when her constant attendants were sixty young Oceanids together with twenty nymphs who looked after her pack of hunting dogs.

Hunting was her first and last love and she imposed chasteness on all her female companions and attendants as a strict rule. So when ZEUS transformed himself into the image of ARTEMIS in order to seduce her companion Callisto, she slew her with arrows to avenge the trickery.

The poor huntsman, Actaeon, unwittingly came across the naked ARTEMIS who was bathing in a pool in the forest. Astonished by her beauty, he briefly paused there but he was seen by the Goddess. Enraged, she transformed Actaeon into a stag and then set her pack of dogs on him and they promptly devoured him.

ORION dared to touch ARTEMIS when they were hunting together and she punished his unsolicited advances by summoning a scorpion which stung ORION on his heel.

The vindictive nature of ARTEMIS is shown when she joined with APOLLO to kill the six sons and the six daughters of Niobe who had commented on the fact that she had produced twelve children against LETO's only two, APOLLO and ARTEMIS.

A certain Admetus, a king of Thessaly, failed to offer a sacrifice to the Goddess on his marriage, only to find that when he entered the bridal chamber it was full of snakes.

Agamemnon and his fleet were stranded due to lack of wind in the port of Aulis. ARTEMIS would restore the wind only on the sacrifice to her of his daughter Iphigenia. However, she took pity on her at the last moment and took her to Tauris where she placed her as chief priestess of the cult of ARTEMIS.

All shipwrecked people on the coast of Tauris were sacrificed to the Goddess when Iphigenia presided. It so happened that Iphigenia's brother, Orestes, landed and was sentenced to death. Iphigenia took Orestes and they ran away, taking with them a statue of ARTEMIS which eventually was placed in a sanctuary at Braurona in eastern Attica, where it was revered as ARTEMIS BRAURONIA, meaning 'of the bear'.

In fact ARTEMIS so venerated the bear that a terrible tale is told. One day, near Athens, a girl was attacked by a bear and her valiant brother killed it. ARTEMIS was so outraged that she sent a plague to Athens. The people consulted the oracle which said that the plague would be removed, provided that every five years a group of little girls between the ages of five and ten were sent to be sacrificed at the temple of ARTEMIS. Human sacrifice and extreme forms of punishment were levied wherever her statue failed to be honoured.

On the other hand, ARTEMIS showed a gentle love of music and often joined her brother APOLLO at Delphi where she sang in the choir of the GRACES and the MUSES.

HERMES

Next in line was HERMES whom the Romans renamed MERCURY. Son of ZEUS and Maia, the daughter of ATLAS, he was born in Arcadia on mount Cyllene, in a deep cave.
Charm, cunning, persuasion, tact and diplomacy all fused to make him the ideal messenger of ZEUS.
He became the God of travellers and thieves. Indeed his son, Autolycus, was to become the master of thievery, under the influence of his father and aided by HERMES' gift to him of invisibility.
He was the God of commerce, both legal and illegal profit and of games of chance.
He was certainly a God of fertility and associated mainly with Goddesses who also represented fertility, the most notable liasion being with APHRODITE, the result of which produced HERMAPHRODITUS. He was also to mate with AMALTHEIA, the goat nymph, and from this union came the God of shepherds, PAN.

He was the God of athletics (his statue stood at the entrance to the stadium at Olympia), and is often depicted as a perfectly proportioned, beautiful young man, wearing a

winged hat and sandals and carrying a magic wand.
He was also responsible for escorting the souls of the dead to the underworld.

The mischievous nature of HERMES manifested itself on the first day he was born when he stole fifty heifers from a herd of cattle belonging to APOLLO. To deceive APOLLO he made the cattle walk backwards and made sandals for his own feet to disguise his footprints. He hid the heifers in a cavern apart from two of them which he skinned and roasted. He then returned to his cradle. APOLLO searched everywhere for the stolen cattle and recruited Silenus and his satyrs, (who were companions of DIONYSUS, and had pointed ears, flat noses and goat's

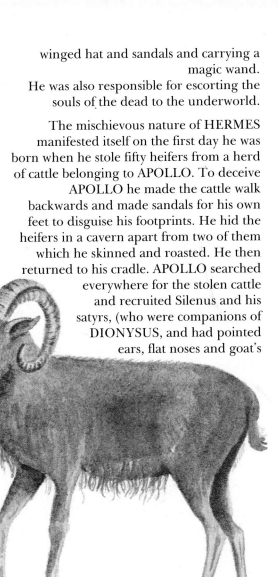

AMALTHEIA

tails), to help in this search, for a reward. The satyrs heard music coming from a cave and were informed by the nympth Cyllene, that a gifted baby boy had recently been born and that she was the nurse. In the cave they found that HERMES had made a musical instrument from a tortoise shell and cowgut. The satyrs noticed two cow hides stretched out in the cave and enquired about the cowgut. HERMES was accused and when APOLLO arrived he recognized the two hides. He took the baby to Olympus and complained to ZEUS about the thievery of his new born son. ZEUS was reluctant to believe such a story but HERMES confessed, telling APOLLO to come with him to the place of hiding and he would return the forty eight heifers.

'Why did you kill two?' enquired APOLLO.

'Because I was hungry, I divided them into twelve equal portions in honour of the twelve great Gods', HERMES answered.'Who is the twelfth God? I know only of eleven', asked APOLLO. 'I, your servant, am the twelfth', said the tactful HERMES.

It was then that APOLLO noticed the musical instrument that HERMES had constructed and was overcome when he heard the beautiful music it produced. It was christened the lyre and APOLLO desired it above all things. HERMES gave the lyre to APOLLO who from that moment became the God of music and APOLLO allowed HERMES to keep the heifers as well as giving him a golden, magic wand. It was also from that moment that HERMES became the protector of herds and flocks and, in this respect, was revered by shepherds and herdsmen throughout Greece. APOLLO and HERMES were to be the closest of friends for ever.

ZEUS was so impressed by the many guiles and aspects of HERMES' nature that he granted him membership of the great Olympian family and HERMES took his place as the personal herald of ZEUS, provided that he gave up telling lies.

'I will never tell lies', he told ZEUS,' although I cannot promise always to tell the truth.'

HERMES was, despite his mischievous nature, a favourite among the Gods and his ingenuity came to their aid on many occasions. He wore HADES' bronze helmet which made him invisible to enable him to slay the giant HIPPOLYTUS during the war of the Giants. His assistance to ZEUS was invaluable. He freed ZEUS from his imprisonment by TYPHOEUS and aided the amorous adventures of ZEUS especially when he killed the giant ARGUS, having lulled him to sleep with his flute, thus freeing Io, who was being persecuted by HERA.

He aided the birth of DIONYSUS and he freed ARES from imprisonment by the Aloadae.

He was always on the side of the Heroes.

When Perseus lost his nerve it was HERMES who gave him new courage.

He accompanied HERACLES to the underworld.

He could induce sleep or awaken from sleep with his magic wand, whichever best served his purpose, and this was his ploy when he made it possible for Priam to recover the body of his son, Hector, from outside the walls of Troy, as recorded in the Iliad.

In the Odyssey, it is said that it was HERMES who gave Odysseus the magic plant which negated the advances of Circe.

It was HERMES who escorted Orpheus on his journey to the underworld to retrieve Eurydice and it was HERMES who reassembled the pieces of Pelops and restored him to life after his father, TANTALUS had cut him up and served him at a banquet for the Gods.

HERMES was the God who brought to men's hearts that which ZEUS desired.

ARES

The seventh in line was ARES, son of ZEUS and HERA. He was to be known to the Romans as MARS and was the God of War. ARES was the least liked son of ZEUS and was likened to his mother HERA by ZEUS who considered him to be obstinate and difficult to manage.

In Homer's Iliad we hear ZEUS addressing ARES thus:

'Of all the Gods who live on Olympus, thou art the most odious to me; for thou enjoyest nothing but strife, war and battles. Thou hast the same obstinate and unmanageable disposition of thy mother HERA, whom I can scarcely control with my words.'

Brutality, towering rages and carnage were his hallmark and he was extremely unpopular with the other Olympian Gods. He was not widely venerated, although temples were dedicated to him in Athens, Olympia and Sparta.

ARES was often in total oppositon to ATHENE where his violent nature was in contrast to her cool and intelligent demeanour. The sight of her would send ARES into a blind rage and finally there was a confrontation. ARES struck ATHENE who retaliated by hurling a great stone at his neck. His knees buckled and he fell to the dust accompanied by the jangling noise of his armour. ATHENE told him:

'Vain fool! Hast thou not yet learned how supreme my strength is to thine?'

He was no more successful in his amorous adventures. APHRODITE, who had married his brother

HEPHAESTUS, was briefly attracted to him and an adulterous affair ensued. The liason, however, was observed by HELIOS, who sees all things, and HEPHAESTUS was informed.

HEPHAESTUS announced that he was going away but in fact went into hiding. The smith God fashioned a net so fine that it could not be seen and so strong that it could not be broken. The net was placed above the couch which ARES normally shared with APHRODITE and when the lovers, after coming together, finally slept, it was dropped, thus enmeshing them.

HEPHAESTUS immediately called for ZEUS and the other Gods to witness the affair of the wife who despised him and the brother who had betrayed him. ARES paid the price for adultery and was banished to the mountains of Thrace.

ARES was normally depicted as a bearded warrior dressed in armour and carrying a large spear. His chariot was drawn by swift horses with golden brow bands.

The imprisoning net

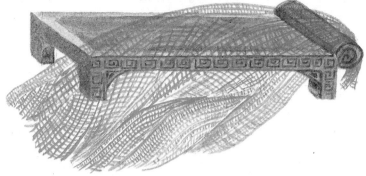

HEPHAESTUS

Eighth after ZEUS came HEPHAESTUS
who was to be adopted later by the Romans
and renamed VULCAN.

HEPHAESTUS was the smith God and the
God of fire and artisans. He was born lame
with a very pronounced and grotesque gait
which often made him the subject of
ridicule by the other Gods. In fact his
mother, HERA, was so ashamed of him that
she threw him from Olympus to earth.
Fortunately he had a soft landing in the sea
where he was found by THETIS and
EURONYME who nurtured
him for nine years in their
underwater grotto which
became for HEPHAESTUS
a workshop as his
incredible skills as a
smith developed.

THETIS the Nereid

Revenge, however,
was in his heart
against his
mother who
had deserted
him and he
fashioned a
very special
golden
chair

which he sent to her as a gift. The moment HERA sat on the chair she became imprisoned in a mechanical locking device and only HEPHAESTUS knew the secret of its unlocking. All the Gods tried unsuccessfully to free HERA. Eventually she was released by her son when he was tricked back to Olympus by DIONYSUS, the God of Wine, who made him very drunk and sent him back draped across a mule. HEPHAESTUS agreed to release his mother on the condition that she arrange his marriage to the beautiful APHRODITE.

HERA established HEPHAESTUS on Olympus with a magnificent workshop which was serviced night and day by twenty bellows. Here he produced golden thrones for his parents and, with the help of the CYCLOPES, he made the famous thunderbolts which were the hallmark of the supremacy of his father, ZEUS. He made the golden chariots for HELIOS and his treacherous brother ARES. He forged POSEIDON's trident and ARIADNE's diadem. He fashioned ATHENE's helmet and armour, ACHILLE's shield and HARMONIA's necklace. From his forge came DEMETER's sickle, Agamemnon's sceptre, HERACLES' cuirass and the golden goblet which ZEUS was to use in his advances towards APHRODITE.
Nothing was impossible to his supreme skill at the forge. He once made, from gold, several mechanical women to assist him at his work. You will remember the gossamer fine net which he forged to trap his brother ARES who lay with his wife APHRODITE, and his creation of the fired clay, namely Pandora, the first mortal woman on whom he placed a golden crown. You will also remember the axe blow that released ATHENE from the head of ZEUS.

HEPHAESTUS became so reconciled to his mother, HERA, that he even dared to intervene on her behalf when, following the rebellion of the Gods, ZEUS had her suspended from the heavens. ZEUS punished the impudent HEPHAESTUS and, taking him by the ankle, hurled him to earth. Poor HEPHAESTUS! For the second time he was thrown from Olympus and he was to be a whole day dropping to earth where he cruelly landed on the island of Lemnos. When later he was reconciled and returned to Olympus, he could only walk with the aid of golden leg supports due to the injuries sustained in that long fall. The poet Milton was later to write:

'from morn
To noon he fell, from noon to dewy eve,
A summer's day, and with the setting sun
Dropt from the zenith, like a falling star,
On Lemnos the Aegean isle.'

The famous volcanoes of Italy, Sicily and the Lipari Islands were known as the workshops of HEPHAESTUS and the constant rumblings of Etna, some say, signify his continuing activity. He was particularly revered on Lemnos. HEPHAESTUS and ATHENE shared temples in Athens. His name possibly derived from HEMERO PHAISTOS or 'he who shines by day', while ATHENE was considered a moon Goddess or 'she who shines by night'. Of course ATHENE was also the patroness of smithcraft and of all mechanical arts.

HEPHAESTUS is often depicted as a bearded figure with a powerful neck, hairy chest and wearing a sleeveless short robe which left his right shoulder bare. On his head was a conical hat such as a blacksmith would wear.

APHRODITE

APHRODITE was ninth in superiority and was the Goddess of feminine beauty. Like HERA, she went every year to the Spring of Canathus at Nauplia, to bathe and renew her

virginity. The Romans adopted her and renamed her 'VENUS', a Goddess of great importance as she was the mother of Aeneas, the founder of Rome.
She was worshipped in Greece as APHRODITE URANIA and as APHRODITE PANDEMOS.
APHRODITE URANIA was originally the 'Goddess of the Sky', but later became the 'Goddess of higher, purer love'. APHRODITE PANDEMOS began as the 'Goddess of all the people', but was eventually worshipped as the 'Goddess of sensual lust'. You will recall the famous judgement of Paris, when APHRODITE used those unashamed sensual characteristics to vanquish HERA and ATHENE in the contest of beauty.
The nature of her birth meant that she was also worshipped as a sea Goddess and the floor of her palace sanctuary at Knossus, in Crete, the centre of Minoan civilisation, was carpeted with shells.
Her magic girdle ensured that everyone was in love with her. She guarded it jealously and was rarely persuaded to lend it to the other Goddesses.
The FATES gave APHRODITE just one divine duty, to make love. However, she was once discovered by ATHENE working on a loom, a craft particularly sacred to ATHENE, and after apologising, vowed that from that day forward she would never turn her hands to work again.

Her great beauty made her the object of desire among the Gods and she was jealously viewed by the other Goddesses. Her unlikely and childless marriage to HEPHAESTUS led her into an adulterous affair with ARES as earlier described, and an affair with HERMES resulted in the birth of a boy, HERMAPHRODITUS. It was this boy who spurned the nymph, Salmacis, causing her to closely embrace him, having asked the Gods to make them one. Her wish was granted and HERMAPHRODITUS became the first person to combine both sexes in one body.

APHRODITE was such a source of distraction to ZEUS that he instilled in her the desire to lie with mortal man. The man was the Trojan shepherd, Anchises, and the baby boy which resulted from the liaison was Aeneas, who was destined to found Rome. Her most notable relationship with mortal man came with her love for ADONIS, who was the child of Smyrna, daughter of King Cinyras of Cyprus.

Smyrna's mother had boasted that her daughter was more beautiful than APHRODITE, who revenged the insult by inducing an illicit relationship between Smyrna and her father when he was drunk. The ensuing pregnancy caused Smyrna to flee from her father, whereupon APHRODITE changed her into a myrrh tree just as she was to be struck by her father's sword. The myrrh tree split from the blow and out tumbled the baby ADONIS.

APHRODITE took the child and concealed him in a chest which she placed in the care of PERSEPHONE, in the underworld, not to be disturbed. PERSEPHONE, however, was curious and discovered ADONIS. She was enraptured with his good looks and brought him up as her own. When APHRODITE learned of this she went to reclaim him but by this time ADONIS had become the lover of PERSEPHONE.

As APHRODITE was herself enamoured by ADONIS, ZEUS was consulted and he referred the judgement to a lower court under the jurisdiction of the muse, CALLIOPE. She decreed that ADONIS should be shared between the two Goddesses but that ADONIS should also have an annual break from their demanding attentions. CALLIOPE therefore further decreed that the year be split into three parts. One third of each year ADONIS would spend with APHRODITE, one third with PERSEPHONE and the third part was for ADONIS to be on his own. APHRODITE disobeyed the judgement. By wearing her magic girdle she enjoyed her share and caused ADONIS to desire her only, during both PERSEPHONES third and his own.

PERSEPHONE reported to ARES who also enjoyed APHRODITE's favours and his revenge was to gore ADONIS to death, disguised as a wild boar, while he was out hunting.

The blood of ADONIS became wild anemones and he descended into Tartarus.

APHRODITE

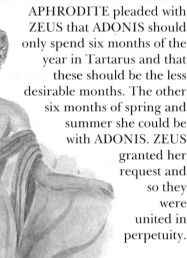

APHRODITE pleaded with ZEUS that ADONIS should only spend six months of the year in Tartarus and that these should be the less desirable months. The other six months of spring and summer she could be with ADONIS. ZEUS granted her request and so they were united in perpetuity.

POSEIDON

Then came POSEIDON, son of CRONUS and RHEA and older brother of ZEUS. He became the God of the sea when, with his brothers ZEUS and HADES, they shared the sky, sea and underworld.

Besides being the God of the sea, he was also God of fresh water and was known as the Earth Shaker when he controlled earthquakes.

The sea was always indicative of his mood. When he was angry it became rough, stirred by his trident and fanned by the winds. When he was content the sea became calm and safe, accompanied by graceful dolphins. In fact POSEIDON is normally depicted carrying a trident, in the company of a dolphin, naked or semi naked and facially looking reasonably like his brother ZEUS.

POSEIDON was married to the nereid, or sea nymph, Amphitrite, which union produced, notably, a son, Triton, and a daughter, Rhode.

Triton was a prophetic merman, half fish and having two tails. He was known as the trumpeter of the sea and used a large shell to produce his music.

Rhode was destined to marry HELIOS and to give her name to the famous sunshine island of Rhodes. A colony of Rhodians built a temple to POSEIDON on the volcanic island of Santorini.

The amorous adventures of POSEIDON almost matched those of ZEUS, and he was lucky that Amphitrite was not of a jealous nature. Only once did she become vindictive, when POSEIDON fell in love with the beautiful nymph, Scilla. The nymph was transformed into a monster as she took a bath when Amphitrite polluted her bath water with a magic potion of herbs.

POSEIDON had a strong relationship with horses. From a metamorphosed union with his sister, DEMETER, was born the wild horse, ARION, while his affair with the one mortal gorgan, Medusa, was to produce PEGASUS, the winged horse on which the Hero, Bellerophon, vanquished the CHIMAERA and attempted to fly to heaven. Possibly the sea and horses combine to explain why today we refer to foam crested waves as 'white horses'.

Generally the offspring of POSEIDON were cruel and violent. By GAEA he produced the giant Antaeus, who became king of Libya and was noted for his cruelty. He built his father a temple from the bones of his victims. By Anippe, a daughter of the river Nile, he produced Busiris, a king of Egypt who killed all strangers who entered that land. Both these sons were later to be put to death by HERACLES.

From a relationship with Melia came Amycus, who was to invent pugilistic contests. This son was killed by the Dioscuri, or twins, CASTOR and POLLUX sons of ZEUS and Leda.

Another offspring, by the nymph Thoosa, was POLYPHEMUS, a Cyclop who was to be blinded by the Hero, Odysseus, in a famous episode from Homer's Odyssey. In revenge, POSEIDON would condemn Odysseus to ten years of persecution on the seas.

Together with HERA and APOLLO, POSEIDON conspired against ZEUS and was punished when the angry God of Gods sentenced him to physically build the walls of Troy.

POSEIDON had many territorial disputes with his fellow Gods, most of which did not result in his favour. He lost Attica to ATHENE, Argos to HERA and Corinth to HELIOS. However, Isthmia was to become his, where he was especially revered with festivals and the famous

Isthmian Games. Perhaps his most famous sanctuary stood on the acropolis at Sounion, in the form of a beautiful marble temple.

POSEIDON was particularly revered by fishermen and mariners in general who all prayed to him for safe journeys.

POSEIDON

HESTIA

HESTIA was the eleventh, the Goddess of the domestic hearth and to be named VESTA by the Romans. A virgin, she did not like the lustful behaviour of APHRODITE and decided to remain chaste, despite the advances of both APOLLO and POSEIDON.

The hearth in both the temples and palaces of the Gods and in the homes of mortal man became the most important feature, where fire was life. When a child was received into the family and given a name, it was common practise, as part of the baptismal ceremony, to run with the child around the hearth. It is interesting to note that a similar action takes place in Greek Orthodox christening ceremonies today, when the godmother walks several times around the baptismal font with the child.

HESTIA

HESTIA was the oldest of the Olympians, the first born of CRONUS and RHEA, and she was respected by all the other Gods. She never exercised her seniority and was content to attempt to maintain the peace of Olympus. She never took part in any disputes or wars and was the most charitable of all the Gods. She represented not only the hearth but the home in general. She invented the art of building and made the family home the natural centre of hospitality to all who might visit. She represented family security and happiness.

HESTIA was venerated through-out Greece where temples had their hearth or altar. ZEUS had decreed that she be the first recipient of any sacrifice.

She was particularly revered at Delphi where its hearth, in the temple of APOLLO, known as the Hestia, was the most important hearth in Greece and indeed the world, as Delphi was thought to signify the centre of the universe.

HESTIA is normally depicted fully robed with a head cloth and shawl. A rare statue of her was in Olympia, probably symbolising the Olympic Spirit.

DEMETER

Finally we have DEMETER, the barley mother who the Romans were to call CERES. She was worshipped throughout Greece perhaps more than any other God or Goddess, mainly because she controlled the very essence of life in the riches and fruits of the earth.
She maintained contact with mortals, teaching them the way, via the legal process, toward becoming civilised.
There were countless temples erected in her honour, called Megara, many of which were situated in forests and she was particularly revered in Attica, Arcadia, the Argolid and Delos. Her cult was mysterious and included orgies within its rituals.

Daughter of CRONUS and RHEA, DEMETER was deceptively seduced by ZEUS and also by POSEIDON, both of whom were her brothers, and she became the mother of KORE and ARION respectively. She was also the mother of PLUTUS, her son by the TITAN, IASION. Her daughter by ZEUS, KORE, became better known as PERSEPHONE, and the Romans were to call her PROSERPINA. The following account represents one of the most famous episodes in Ancient Greek Mythology and probably accounts in no small way for DEMETER's popularity as Goddess of the fertile and cultivated soil.

DEMETER had an overwhelming love for her daughter and she became distraught with worry when KORE was

abducted, whilst picking flowers, and taken
to the underworld by HADES. In fact
HADES manifested himself
from a particularly beautiful narcissus
which the girl was about to pick.

For nine days DEMETER searched far and
wide for
her
daughter
and finally
knew of

DEMETER

HADES' despicable act from the observant HELIOS. At this point, DEMETER left Olympus in despair and disguising herself as an old woman, she drifted from town to town until she finally arrived at Eleusis, where she sought a position as a servant or nurse.
She became nurse to a baby boy called Demophoon, son of a King Celeus and his wife, Metaneira.

In the course of bringing up the boy, DEMETER anointed him with ambrosia and began the process of purging him with the open fire in order to destroy his mortality and make him a God. She was, however, discovered by Metaneira and the transition from human to God was not complete. In order to explain her act, DEMETER was forced to reveal herself and so both her name and her divinity were discovered. A temple was raised in her honour. DEMETER then gave the knowledge of agriculture to Triptolemus, the brother of Demophoon, and sent him out as her disciple to visit and teach the art to all Greece and the surrounding areas. DEMETER's distress over the abduction of her daughter KORE became even more acute and so she brought about a cruel and harsh year on earth, when no crops grew from a barren soil. ZEUS and all the other Gods implored her to restore fertility to the earth but she said that she would only do so if she could see KORE again.
ZEUS, therefore, sent his messenger, HERMES, to see HADES, with orders to return with his daughter, KORE, who by this time had been renamed PERSEPHONE. Her release was granted by HADES, but, before she left, he tricked her into eating some pomegranate seeds which had the effect of forming an indissoluble, binding union between them.
DEMETER was overcome with joy to see her daughter but sorrow returned when she learned of the pomegranate

seeds. ZEUS brought about a compromise. PERSEPHONE was to spend one third of each year in the Underworld with HADES and two thirds on earth with her mother.

And so the seasons were born, whereby the earth would be barren when PERSEPHONE was with HADES, the winter, and when she returned to DEMETER on earth, the crops would grow; spring and summer would arrive.

This episode was to become the heart of the Eleusian Mysteries, a series of festivals held in Eleusis and Athens in honour of the great power of their own revered DEMETER and KORE. Only Greek speakers could be initiated into the secret rituals, although during the Imperial period, certain Roman Emperors were allowed to participate.

DEMETER is normally represented as sombre beauty, often seated, dressed in long robes, holding in her hands the cereals of the earth.

THE LESSER GODS

We cannot conclude our Guide to the Greek Gods without dealing with the lesser Gods, and in order to detail them in a logical manner, we will place them in two categories, namely:

The Minor Gods on Olympus and the Attendant Divinities,
and The Gods of the Underworld and their executors.

We begin with:

THE MINOR GODS
ON OLYMPUS

Chart 8

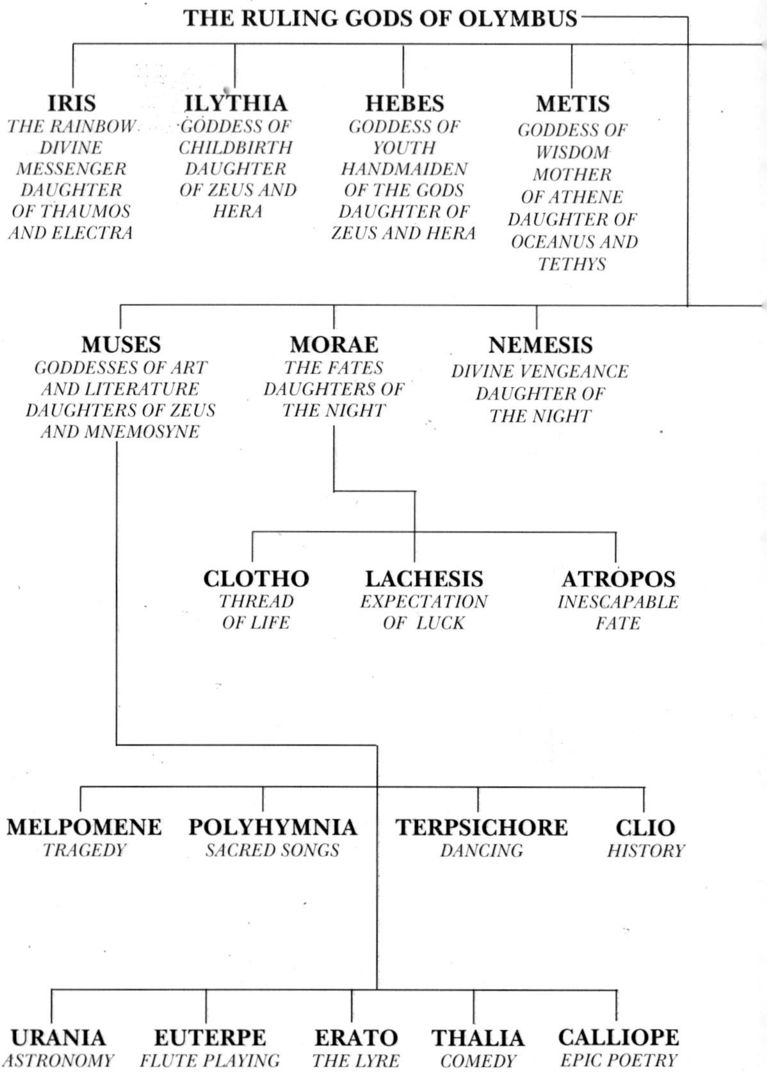

THE RULING GODS OF OLYMBUS

IRIS
*THE RAINBOW
DIVINE
MESSENGER
DAUGHTER
OF THAUMOS
AND ELECTRA*

ILYTHIA
*GODDESS OF
CHILDBIRTH
DAUGHTER
OF ZEUS AND
HERA*

HEBES
*GODDESS OF
YOUTH
HANDMAIDEN
OF THE GODS
DAUGHTER OF
ZEUS AND HERA*

METIS
*GODDESS OF
WISDOM
MOTHER
OF ATHENE
DAUGHTER OF
OCEANUS AND
TETHYS*

MUSES
*GODDESSES OF ART
AND LITERATURE
DAUGHTERS OF ZEUS
AND MNEMOSYNE*

MORAE
*THE FATES
DAUGHTERS OF
THE NIGHT*

NEMESIS
*DIVINE VENGEANCE
DAUGHTER OF
THE NIGHT*

CLOTHO
*THREAD
OF LIFE*

LACHESIS
*EXPECTATION
OF LUCK*

ATROPOS
*INESCAPABLE
FATE*

MELPOMENE
TRAGEDY

POLYHYMNIA
SACRED SONGS

TERPSICHORE
DANCING

CLIO
HISTORY

URANIA
ASTRONOMY

EUTERPE
FLUTE PLAYING

ERATO
THE LYRE

THALIA
COMEDY

CALLIOPE
EPIC POETRY

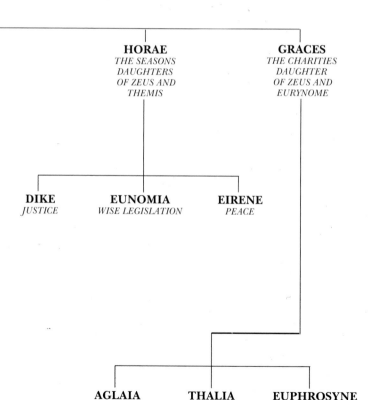

THEMIS
GODDESS OF LAW.
DAUGHTER OF
GAEA AND
URANUS

DIONYSUS
GOD OF WINE
ROMAN
BACCHUS.SON OF
ZEUS AND
SEMELE

PAN
GOD OF
SHEPHERDS SON
OF HERMES AND
AMALTHEIA

ASCLEPIUS
GOD OF
MEDICINE
ROMAN.
AESCULAPIUS
SON OF APOLLO
AND CORONIS

HORAE
THE SEASONS
DAUGHTERS
OF ZEUS AND
THEMIS

GRACES
THE CHARITIES
DAUGHTER
OF ZEUS AND
EURYNOME

DIKE
JUSTICE

EUNOMIA
WISE LEGISLATION

EIRENE
PEACE

AGLAIA
SPLENDOR

THALIA
GOOD CHEER

EUPHROSYNE
MIRTH

Chart No 8 shows the eight most important minor Gods, together with the attendant Divinities, namely the FATES, SEASONS, GRACES and MUSES, who were there to serve all of the Gods, all of the time.

The Minor Gods were, in order of seniority:

THEMIS
METIS
DIONYSUS
PAN
HEBE
ILYTHIA
IRIS
ASCLEPIUS

THEMIS

THEMIS, the daughter of GAEA and URANUS, was the Goddess of Law and the keeper of Order. She was a prophetess and some say that she had the Delphic oracle after GAEA, passing it later to APOLLO.

She was the guardian of oaths and the personification of Justice.
She laid down the divine law, which differentiated between right and wrong, and was always on hand to advise ZEUS in his judgements.

She organised all the meetings of the Gods with her agendas and minutes, the divine company secretary.

She was the only original TITANESS to be honoured on Olympus, while on earth she became known as SOTEIRA, the protectress, who protected the innocent and punished the guilty.
Her cult was widespread, with a temple consecrated to her

THEMIS

in Athens. Together with ZEUS she was worshipped at sanctuaries, in particular those at Troezen, Olympia and Thebes.

It was THEMIS who was to advise DEUCALION and his wife, PYRRHA, on the re-peopling of the earth, following the deluge that ZEUS sent to destroy mankind. DEUCALION, the son of PROMETHEUS, was the Greek 'Noah', who on his father's instructions, built an ark. He and PYRRHA, the daughter of EPIMETHEUS, rode out the flood and were eventually grounded.

It was then that THEMIS, in a divine message, told them to take their mother's bones and throw them over their shoulders. They realised that this must mean the stones of the earth and they threw them, as instructed. Those thrown by DEUCALION became men and those thrown by PYRRHA, women.

THEMIS is normally depicted as a solemn figure with a stern countenance, holding the famous pair of scales, which we still associate today with the weighing of right versus wrong.

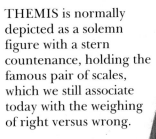

METIS

METIS

METIS, the Goddess of Wisdom, was the daughter of OCEANUS and TETHYS.

As Hesiod was to record, she:

'knew more things than all the Gods and men put together'.

You will recall that it was METIS who

dispensed the draught that made CRONUS disgorge the brothers and sisters of ZEUS.

And of course it was METIS who was to become the mother of ATHENE, having been swallowed by her husband, ZEUS, when pregnant, in order to thwart the oracle of GAEA, which had proclaimed that a second offspring would be a boy who would be more powerful than the God.

This action gave ZEUS supreme wisdom because METIS became part of ZEUS and continued to counsel him from within for ever more.

DIONYSUS

DIONYSUS was the son of ZEUS and Semele and the Romans called him BACCHUS. He was the God of Wine and so a very popular God because he was associated with festivals and joy. However, his cult became enthused to a remarkable degree. Women abandoned their household chores, beat drums and danced themselves into an orgiastic trance, and when in this state, they could tear apart and devour both animals and humans. They donned the skins of fauns over their robes, crowned themselves with ivy leaves and wore grotesque masks, DIONYSUS being represented by a bull mask. These women followers were known as Bacchantes or Maenads.

The God also had masculine followers, who behaved in a wild, drunken manner at their rituals. Notably they were: SATYRS, or goat men, with cloven hooves and tails, and: SILENI, or horse men, hairy and with horses ears, tails and legs.

Both the SATYRS and the SILENI were wild spirits and demons who worshipped the vine and practised fertility rites.

The extreme frenzy of these rituals was eventually quietened by APOLLO, who then brought DIONYSUS to govern with him at DELPHI.

Evidence has shown that DIONYSUS was particularly revered by the Minoans who worshipped the bull.

The birth of DIONYSUS

The mother of DIONYSUS had been killed, when she was six month's pregnant, by HERA, in revenge for the infidelity of ZEUS. But ZEUS had rescued the infant and, within the thigh of his own body, had completed the gestation period until DIONYSUS was born. ZEUS asked HERMES to look after his son and he was placed in the care of the nymphs, who brought him up, becoming, in the process, his ardent followers. They were known as the nymphs of Nysa, but as every region that worshipped him claimed to have a place called Nysa, it was never known where it actually was.

DIONYSUS was to travel far and wide to introduce the vine and convert mortal man to his worship. Numerous tales exist of his exploits. He was kidnapped by pirates and tied to their ship's mast. He turned the sea into wine and the sails of the ship into a grape vine. He changed himself into an awesome lion which caused the pirates to jump overboard in terror. As soon as they hit the wine sea, they were transformed into dolphins.

As we might expect, the God had a very active love life and perhaps his most important love was for the lovely ARIADNE, the daughter of King Minos of Crete. ARIADNE had been deserted on the island of Naxos by the hero Theseus, to be discovered by DIONYSUS who fell in love with her. They were married and at the request of her husband, ZEUS made ARIADNE immortal. The pair had three daughters, namely INOPIONAS, EVANTHES and STAPHYLOS, who all devoted themselves to the cultivation of the vine.

DIONYSUS is usually represented as a youth, beautiful, slightly effeminate, reclining on a couch, with ivy leaves crowning his long, curly hair and clutching a wine goblet in one hand and with a magic stick, the 'thyrsus', in the other. When he touched somebody with this 'thyrsus', he injected them with a contagious and wild madness.

Goats were especially associated with the sacrifices dedicated to DIONYSUS and certain illustrations give him the goat's horns to perhaps accentuate the devilish properties of alcohol. His cult followers practised mainly at night.

Festivals in his honour were held all over Greece, perhaps the most famous in Athens when his statue was carried from his temple to the slopes of the Acropolis, which housed his theatre. (This theatre is the oldest known in Greece, and is still to be seen). A huge following danced around his statue and hymns were sung, accompanied by flutes, all the way to the theatre where competitions were held to find the very best poems, tragedies and comedies. It was here that the famous Sophocles. Aeschylus, Euripides and Aristophanes displayed their talents.

It was Euripides who wrote the 'Bacchae', a tragedy ever popular today, which tells the story of the arrival of DIONYSUS and his wild followers at Thebes. He had gone there to introduce himself and recruit the inhabitants to his worship. He was rejected by Pentheus, King of Thebes, who insulted and attempted to imprison the God, but DIONYSUS had already mesmerized the women of Thebes, including the mother of Pentheus, Agave, who were all dancing wildly on a nearby mountain. Pentheus was induced to spy on this ritual, was seen, and was torn to pieces. Agave eventually returned with his head, only to discover, when the madness subsided, that she was holding the head of her son.

Another story relates the visit of the God to Argos, where he bewildered those who failed to recognise his divinity and in their insane state, they devoured their own children.

At Orchomenus, the three daughters of the king refused to take part in his festival. DIONYSUS terrified them and eventually transformed them into a mouse, an owl and a screeching owl..

PAN

PAN, the son of HERMES and AMALTHIA, was the God of the shepherds and flocks. He inherited his two-legged, goat shape from his mother, having a human torso, with the

legs, ears and horns of a goat.
An amorous God, he controlled the fertility of the flocks,

which accounts for his predominantly phallic representations. His natural abode was the forest and he is normally associated with the countryside of Arcadia. He was a protector of the olive and the vine, and he taught the art of bee-keeping.

He delighted in playing with the wood nymphs, who he could both charm and terrify at will. The poet, Elizabeth Barrett Browning was to write of him:

'What was he doing, the great God PAN,
Down in the reeds by the river?
Spreading ruin and scattering ban,
Splashing and paddling with hooves of a goat,
And breaking the golden lilies afloat,
With the dragon fly on the river.'

One day he was chasing the nymph, SYRINX, daughter of LADON, the river God, when she cried out to her father to save her, which he did by changing her into a reed. In despair, PAN cut the reed and fashioned it into a musical instrument, the syrinx, but better known by us all as the Pan Pipes, and still in use today by shepherds in Greece.

PAN loved the nymph, PITYS, who preferred him to the amorous advances of BOREAS, the north wind. In his anger, BOREAS crushed PITYS against a rock, but GAEA transformed the unfortunate nymph into the fragrant pine tree.

PAN had the power to induce a 'panic' terror when required and you will remember how he used this to help free ZEUS from the monster, TYPHOEUS.

He was associated with dreams, especially the nightmare. He would haunt those who disturbed him from his slumbers, particularly at midday when he most liked to sleep.

Before the famous battle of Marathon, PAN appeared to the Athenians and promised to defeat the Persians, provided they would worship him in Athens. After their victory, the Athenians built a sanctuary to him on the Acropolis, which became the centre of his worship.

PAN was to be strongly associated with DIONYSUS, because they jointly

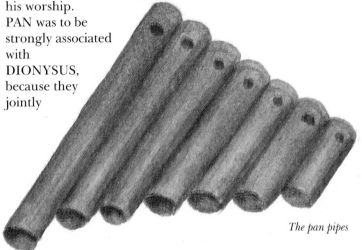

The pan pipes

represented the power of the vine and the frenzies that it induced.

On Olympus, PAN became the court jester and provided much entertainment for the Gods with his comic and mischievous antics.

HEBE

HEBE, the Goddess of Youth, was the daughter of ZEUS and HERA, and sister to ILYTHIA, ARES and HEPHAESTUS.

Blessed with eternal youth, she carried out

mainly domestic functions on Olympus.

She dispensed the ambrosia and nectar to the other Gods until this duty was given to GANYMEDE, a mortal boy of great beauty who was brought by the eagle of ZEUS to Olympus,

where he still waits on the Gods.

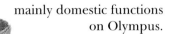

Ambrosia and nectar

The many duties of HEBE included the preparation of HERA's chariot and horses when a journey was intended. She assisted ARES in his toilet and dress.

But perhaps her greatest claim to fame was that she became the wife of the illustious Hero, HERACLES, when he became a God and took his place on Olympus. They were to have two children, ANICETUS and ALEXIARES.

ILYTHIA

ILYTHIA was the Goddess of Childbirth and a daughter of ZEUS and HERA. No child could be born unless she was present, where she aided the birth and relieved the birth pain.

You will remember how HERA delayed her, for nine days, from attending the desperate LETO, who was to give birth to APOLLO and ARTEMIS. In fact HERA used the same delaying tactics when ALCMENE gave birth to HERACLES. ILYTHIA was particularly associated with Crete, and her cult is recorded on a tablet found at Knossos.

ILYTHIA
attends a birth

Together with ARTEMIS, she presided over all aspects of childbirth and is often duplicated with her mother HERA in the functions of marriage and the sexual lives of women.

The Romans were to know her as LUCINA (light), or JUNO LUCINA, where she was the deity who made a child see the light of day. She is normally depicted in a kneeling position, giving with one hand a gesture of encouragement, while the other holds a torch aloft, thus signifying her attendance on a birth.

IRIS

IRIS, the Goddess of the Rainbow, was the wife of the west wind, ZEPHYRUS, the daughter of THAUMUS and ELECTRA and a sister of the HARPIES.
She was a divine messenger of the Gods, particularly of HERA and ZEUS, where the rainbow was

IRIS

seen to connect the heavens to the earth with its glorious spectrum of colour.

Always travelling alone when on her numerous errands, she was often waylaid by CENTAURS or SATYRS.

To HERA, she was a handmaiden who prepared the bath, assisted with the toilet and constantly tended her every comfort. Ever good natured, she would find the winds whenever her assistance was required, such as by becalmed ships.

IRIS was particularly revered on Delos, presumably for the part she played in eventually bringing ILYTHIA to attend the birth of APOLLO and ARTEMIS, and here, offerings of honey, dried figs and wheat cakes were made to her.

Normally depicted wearing a full tunic, she held a herald's staff. Her hair was adorned by a golden band and she was winged, as were her shoes.

ASCLEPIUS

Son of APOLLO and Coronis, ASCLEPIUS was the God of Healing, whom the Romans would call AESCULAPIUS.

You will remember that APOLLO had been offended when Coronis married a mortal, Ischys, when she was already with child by APOLLO. This child was ASCLEPIUS, who was removed from the dead body of his mother after she had been killed by the arrows of ARTEMIS. The baby was placed in the care of CHIRON, the Centaur, the wise son of CRONUS, who lived on Mount Pelion.
CHIRON was renowned for his knowledge of medicine and he taught ASCLEPIUS all he knew. However, ASCLEPIUS' learning of the art knew no bounds and his fame spread with every remarkable cure. His worship spread throughout Greece and over 300 sites have been located where healing sanctuaries were established, run by priests

who were devotees of the cult of the God. Sick people flocked to these sanctuaries, where on arrival, the pilgrim was introduced to the following instruction written over the entrance:

'When you enter the abode of the God, which smells of incense, you must be pure, and thought is pure when you think with piety.'

The pilgrim then had to bathe as a purification of the body,

and to drink from the sacred spring in order to purify the soul. Then, following the Sacred Way, he was led to the Temple of ASCLEPIUS, where nearby was an altar. Here, a sacrifice was offered to 'APOLLO and ASCLEPIUS' and this could range from an ox to a simple fruit, depending on the wealth of the pilgrim. Religious rites followed, and a state of auto suggestion was induced when ASCLEPIUS would appear to the sick in their dreams and the miracle cure would be passed to them.

ASCLEPIUS' achievements were to work against him when HADES complained to ZEUS that he was being deprived of too many souls, owing to the life prolonging treatments of ASCLEPIUS. It was even rumoured that he had resurrected the dead. Indeed this had been the case when Hippolytus, the son of the hero, Theseus, was given fresh life.

This power to overcome nature caused ZEUS to strike ASCLEPIUS with a thunderbolt, following which he was admitted to Olympus at APOLLO's request and took his place with the great ruling Gods.

As time passed, faith in the God diminished somewhat and the sanctuaries, whilst remaining religious centres with devotion to the God, developed into more sophisticated medical establishments.

Priests became practising physicians and incorporated with the medicine and surgery was the provision of a còmplex of gymnasiums, athletic stadiums, baths and theatres. These all combined to assist the total cure of both mind and body.

ASCLEPIUS had three daughters, known as HYGEIA, the Goddess of Health, PANAKEIA, which name denoted 'cure all', and IASO, meaning healing.

There were also two sons named PODALEIRIUS and

MACHAON, who were to become skilful healers who tended the injured in the battle of Troy.

The major sanctuary to ASCLEPIUS was situated in a beautiful and serene setting at Epidauros, in the Argolid region of the Peloponnese. Visited by millions over the years, it still houses the best preserved and acoustically perfect theatre which seats 14,000 people and annually presents a festival of works by the great Greek playwrights.

ASCLEPIUS was normally depicted standing, wearing a loose robe and holding a staff on which a snake was entwined. Facially he resembled ZEUS, with long hair and a beard.
The snake was sacred to him and was used extensively in his famous cures. In modern days the snake has become our own medical symbol.

The staff of ASCLEPIUS

THE ATTENDANT DIVINITIES

THE MOIRAE or FATES

Created by NIGHT, the white robed FATES were birth spirits, who appeared on the third night after a birth and allotted the length, fortune and inevitability of the new baby's life.

They numbered three, and they were representative, also, of the Triple Moon Goddess. The word MOERA meant 'phase' and this moon Goddess depicted the three phases of the moon, so we can view them thus:

The New Moon, or maiden Goddess, the first period of one's years.

The Full Moon, or nymph Goddess, the second period of one's life, and

The Old Moon, or crone Goddess, the last period of one's years.

These three FATES were known, you will remember, as:

CLOTHO, the spinner, with her loom and thread, who personified the length of life which was allotted to a person at birth. LACHESIS, who apportioned to a person the share of luck or fortune that was his right to expect, and ATROPOS, who made sure that the thread of life was cut at the end of the allotted span; man's inescapable destiny, for there could be no appeal.

NEMESIS

NEMESIS, created by NIGHT, was known as the Divine Vengeance. She would punish any mortal who displeased the Gods by offending their moral laws or by exciting their jealousy with excessive riches or even happiness.
She preserved the balance of the human condition. She was responsible for ensuring that law and order were maintained. She is sometimes shown with a finger to her mouth, suggesting that silence is the best course if you are not to attract the divine anger.
NEMESIS was the personification of righteous indignation whenever human presumption offended the Gods.

THE HORAE, or Goddesses of the Seasons

From the marriage of ZEUS and THEMIS came the HORAE. From their mother they inherited the qualities of justice. They were:
EUNOMIA, Goddess of wise legislation or good government,
DIKE, Goddess of justice or right, and
EIRENE, Goddess of peace.
However, some accounts strangely link them with the regularity of the seasons. Three in number, they represented the tripartite Greek year which consisted of Spring, Summer and Winter and is still recognized today. With the power to make beings and plants grow, they were revered by peasants and were very welcome guests at the birth and wedding ceremonies of both Gods and Heroes. They were often in the company of APHRODITE, DIONYSUS, PAN and DEMETER, being similarly associated with fertility.
Athens, Argos and Olympia were particularly important centres of worship of the HORAE.

THE CHARITIES or GRACES

Goddesses of Beauty and Charm, according to Hesiod they were the three daughters of ZEUS and EURYNOME. They were named:

AGLAIA, Goddess of radiant splendour,

The CHARITIES

EUPHROSYNE, Goddess of joy and mirth, and THALIA, Goddess of good cheer.

Like the HORAE, they were also associated with fertility in all its aspects and their particular attributes naturally led them to be attendants to APHRODITE.

The joyful arrival of Spring, with its blaze of flowers, was especially attributed to the CHARITIES and they were sure to be present whenever and wherever celebrations or feasts took place, in order to ensure that happiness and good humour would have their places at the table.

Pindar was to say about them:

'With you, all becomes sweetness and charm'.

Normally depicted as young, beautiful and naked young women, they were particularly revered in Orchomenus, in Boeotia, and had two sanctuaries in Athens.

THE MUSES

These were the Goddesses of the Arts and Literature and were the daughters of ZEUS over his Titaness aunt, MNEMOSYNE, the personofication of memory.

It is said that following the victory of ZEUS over the TITANS he was asked, by the other Gods, to celebrate and honour the epic struggle by establishing divinities that would broaden the mind. ZEUS lay with MNEMOSYNE for nine nights and the combination of their special intelligence produced the nine MUSES. They were:

CLIO

CLIO was the Goddess of History, and her attributes were the trumpet and instrument which measured time, proportional to the flow of water. It was known as a clepsydra.

CLIO also had a tragic connection with a flower, the

hyacinth. She was foolish enough to criticise APHRODITE's love affair with ADONIS. As a punishment, APHRODITE instilled an all consuming desire within CLIO for the King of Macedonia, Pierus, and she had a beautiful son by him, called Hyacinth. This child became the dearest friend and companion of APOLLO. In a friendly contest, it was APOLLO's discus that fatally struck Hyacinth on the forehead. APOLLO was distraught, and Hyacinth's body and flowing blood were reborn as the beautiful flower. It is said that APOLLO marked the petals with the Greek letters ᾽AX, which together mean 'alas'.

It is said that the king, Pierus, also had nine daughters, called the Pierides, who challenged the MUSES to a poetry contest. For their impertinence and because the MUSES were special companions of APOLLO, God of music, he changed the Pierides into magpies.

CLIO is normally depicted seated, along with her sister, URANIA.

EUTERPE

EUTERPE was the Goddess of the flute and music associated with this instrument.

She had a son, Rhesus, by STRYMON, the river God of Thrace. An oracle stated that if the horses of Rhesus were to drink the waters of the river Xanthus, during the siege of Troy, then Troy would become invincible. To forestall this prediction, Odysseus and Diomedes killed Rhesus.

THALIA

The Goddess of comedy, THALIA was especially connected with shepherds and their pastoral environment. Hence her depiction, carrying the shepherd's staff and the now famous comic mask.

THALIA was loved by ZEUS and her twin sons were the PALICI, or the Dioscuri of Sicily.

MELPOMENE

MELPOMENE was the Goddess of tragedy and hers the tragic mask. It is said that she furnished HERACLES with his club.

By the river god, ACHELOUS, she had the Sirens, and you will hear more of them in our tales of the Heroes.

MELPOMENE

TERPSICHORE

The Goddess of dance and of lyric poetry, to TERPSICHORE is attributed the stringed instrument called a cithara, the ancient version of our modern guitar.

ERATO

ERATO was the Goddess of the lyre and of love poetry. She had a son, Thamyris, who became a famous Delphian musician and poet, winning many constests. However, he had the audacity to challenge his mother and aunts, and he paid the price by being blinded and made dumb.

URANIA

The Goddess of astronomy, URANIA's special attributes were the globe and the compass.

Together with APOLLO, she produced Linus, the inventor of rhythm and melody. Unfortunately, Linus was rash enough to challenge his father, the God of music, to a song contest, paying for his arrogance with his life. This Goddess is normally depicted in a sitting position.

POLYHYMNIA

This is the Goddess of sacred song and the art of mimic. She was the classic MUSE, always depicted in an attitude of deep thought and with her finger to her mouth.

CALLIOPE

CALLIOPE was the Goddess of epic poetry and eloquence. Her attributes were the tablet and the stylus.

By APOLLO she had two sons, HYMANAEUS and IALEMUS, but it was by Oeagrus, King of Thrace, that she bore Orpheus, the most famous musician and poet of all. Orpheus, given the lyre by APOLLO and trained by the MUSES, could even make rocks and trees move and follow his music. Wild animals were bewitched by his melodious notes.

It was Orpheus who joined Jason and the Argonauts, as you will read in the stories of the Greek Heroes, but his most famous adventure was his descent into Tartarus to recover Eurydice, whom he had lost when she died of a snake bite. With his music, Orpheus enchanted CHARON, the ferryman, in order to cross the river, styx. He then made CERBERUS, the three headed monster dog, docile with his lyre and his music finally softened even the heart of HADES. HADES released Eurydice to Orpheus on condition that he should not look back until they were safely out of the Underworld.

It was only when Orpheus saw daylight that he lapsed and glanced back, to ensure that Eurydice was still safely with him. Alas, poor Eurydice was gone forever.

The unfortunate Orpheus fell foul of DIONYSUS when he became the disciple of APOLLO, rather than the God of Wine. As a punishment, DIONYSUS set the frenzied Bacchae or Maeneds on to Orpheus as he preached in the temple of APOLLO. Orpheus was torn to pieces, and it is said that his head continued to sing as it floated down the river Hebrus, towards the open sea.

The MUSES were distraught at the fate of Orpheus. They collected his head and limbs, burying them at the foot of Mount Olympus where nightingales now sing sweetly.

THE GODS OF THE
UNDERWORLD
and their executors

Chart 9

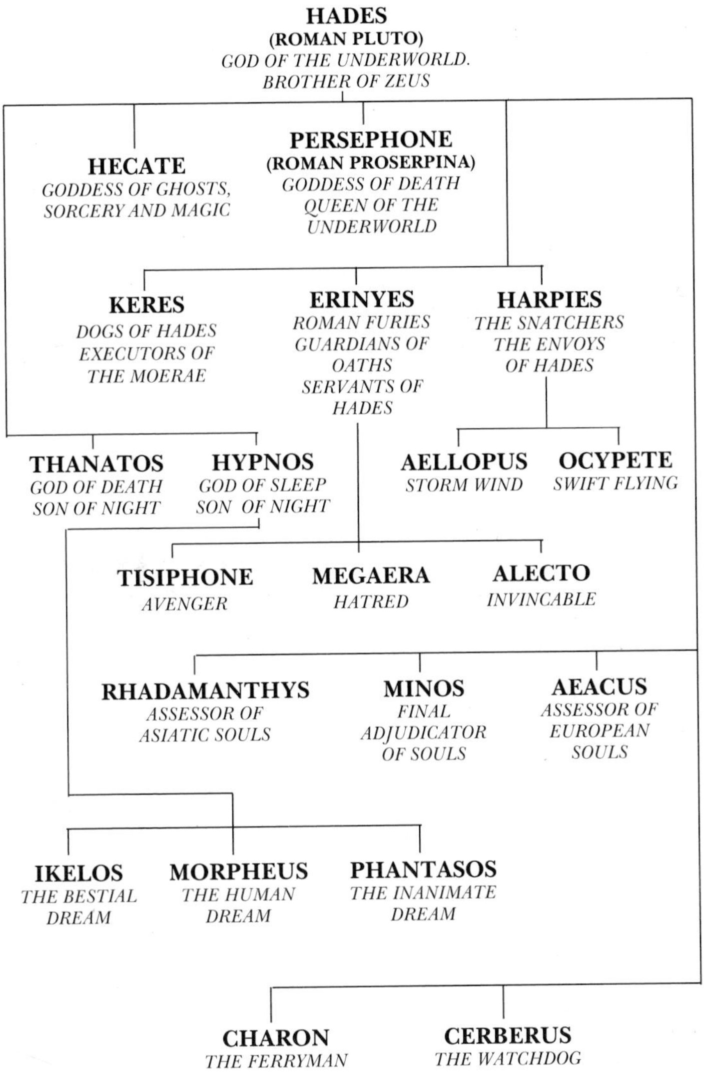

HADES
(ROMAN PLUTO)
GOD OF THE UNDERWORLD.
BROTHER OF ZEUS

HECATE
GODDESS OF GHOSTS,
SORCERY AND MAGIC

PERSEPHONE
(ROMAN PROSERPINA)
GODDESS OF DEATH
QUEEN OF THE
UNDERWORLD

KERES
DOGS OF HADES
EXECUTORS OF
THE MOERAE

ERINYES
ROMAN FURIES
GUARDIANS OF
OATHS
SERVANTS OF
HADES

HARPIES
THE SNATCHERS
THE ENVOYS
OF HADES

THANATOS
GOD OF DEATH
SON OF NIGHT

HYPNOS
GOD OF SLEEP
SON OF NIGHT

AELLOPUS
STORM WIND

OCYPETE
SWIFT FLYING

TISIPHONE
AVENGER

MEGAERA
HATRED

ALECTO
INVINCIBLE

RHADAMANTHYS
ASSESSOR OF
ASIATIC SOULS

MINOS
FINAL
ADJUDICATOR
OF SOULS

AEACUS
ASSESSOR OF
EUROPEAN
SOULS

IKELOS
THE BESTIAL
DREAM

MORPHEUS
THE HUMAN
DREAM

PHANTASOS
THE INANIMATE
DREAM

CHARON
THE FERRYMAN

CERBERUS
THE WATCHDOG

Finally, we come to the Underworld.

It was originally believed that the earth was flat, constrained by an encircling river, which had to be crossed in order to reach the underworld, which was a barren waste where no mortal could survive. Without the sun, no leaves or fruits adorned the black trees and the only plant which grew was the asphodel, which on earth was associated with barren ground, cemeteries and ruins.

This region existed in the very centre of the earth, shrouded in shadows and mystery, and was known as EREBUS.

There were few entrance points to the underworld and they were mainly via subterranean rivers, such as the Acheron and the Cocytus, whose names meant sadness and lamentation respectively.

The three regions of EREBUS were Tartarus, Elysium and the Asphodel fields.

Tartarus was reserved for the evil beings who had committed crimes against, or offended, the moral laws of the Gods. Here they would suffer everlasting tortures. It was here that you would find the giant, TITYUS, constantly ravaged by two vultures, along with TANTALUS and his starvation from both food and drink and, of course, the TITANS.

Elysium was the resting place of the various children of the Gods and the souls of the just. It was a happy place, free from inclement weather, a restful haven, where peace reigned. The sombre Asphodel fields was the region reserved for all those who were neither virtuous nor evil. When committed to the underworld, the treacherous river Styx had to be crossed and it was here that old CHARON, the miserly ferryman, would take the dead across in his crazy boat, but only if the fare was paid, usually with a coin which had been placed under the tongue. Arrive without the fare and you would be destined to wait eternally on the bank of the river.

Once across, on the far bank was the Grove of PERSEPHONE, Queen of the Underworld, which led to the gate of the kingdom of HADES, guarded by the three headed hound of hell, CERBERUS.

CERBERUS would playfully greet the dead with much wagging of his tail, but once through the gate there was no return and only HERMES, HERACLES and Orpheus found the way to appease CERBERUS in order to leave this nether region.

Souls were judged, at this point, by a tribunal, consisting of the president, HADES, and his three assessors, namely MINOS, RHADAMANTHYS and AEACUS. You will remember that RHADAMANTHYS and MINOS were the sons of ZEUS and EUROPA, while AEACUS was the son of ZEUS and the nymph AEGINA. RHADAMANTHYS tried the Asiatics, AEACUS the Europeans and they both consulted MINOS over any difficulties. Dependant on the outcome, the path of no return would lead the evil to TARTARUS, the virtuous to Elysium and those who fell into neither category, to the Asphodel fields.

HADES

HADES, whom the Romans were to call PLUTO, was the God of the Underworld, son of CRONUS and RHEA and brother of ZEUS and POSEIDON.

He was a major God who chose not to take his place on Olympus, rarely leaving his underground Kingdom.

While he was a stern, even gloomy God, he was never considered to be evil. He dealt fairly with the arriving souls and very rarely altered the decisions of his tribunal of assessors, MINOS, RHADAMANTHYS and AECUS.

On the few occasions that he did relent, it had to be ZEUS himself who made the request, which was never a command. When ZEUS, needing assistance in the war against the TITANS, requested the release of the CYCLOPES, HADES was rewarded by the one-eyed giants with a helmet, called a 'kini' which, when worn, made him invisible.

HADES did not torment the dead, a task reserved for the ERINYES or FURIES, who were his servants or messengers. He was associated with his sister, DEMETER, regarding the fertility of the soil, and all the products of the earth, both vegetable and mineral, were considered to be gifts from him. It was these gifts that allowed people to prosper, therefore the other name often used for him was PLUTO, meaning the rich one, and it was this name that the Romans adopted for him.

Living in the Underworld, HADES had far less opportunity to satisfy his amorous inclinations than his brothers. In order to secure a wife, he abducted KORE, the daughter of his brother, ZEUS, and his sister, DEMETER, and made her the Queen of the Underworld, where she was renamed PERSEPHONE. You have already read about this famous episode which led to the seasonal fertility of the soil.

On a rare visit to earth, he pursued a beautiful nymph, called Minthe, which led his mother in law, DEMETER, to crush Minthe to death. HADES transformed her into a plant, the much used and fragrant mint.

His only other love was for LEUCE, the daughter of OCEANUS. HADES brought her to the Underworld, only for her to die in the subterranean gloom. HADES turned her into a white poplar tree which grew profusely in Elysium, where souls of the virtuous enjoyed their permanent retirement.

The narcissus and the cypress were both
sacred to him and sacrifices to HADES
would normally be the black ram.
His main centre of worship on earth was at
Eleusis, where together with DEMETER
and PERSEPHONE, the mysterious rites
were strongly
connected with his
powers.

HADES

PERSEPHONE

Daughter of ZEUS and DEMETER, wife of
HADES, PERSEPHONE was Queen of the
Underworld and the Goddess of the Dead.
The Romans would alter her name to
PROSERPINA.
The story of PERSEPHONE has already
been adequately covered in earlier chapters
and few tales relate to PERSEPHONE, as
on earth she was virtually one with her

mother, DEMETER, and was therefore especially revered in Athens and Eleusis.

Her Greek name meant 'bringer of destruction', and her Roman name meant 'the fearful one', but this is not indicative of her nature, which could often be gentle and considerate. Indeed it was in response to DIONYSUS' gift of myrtle that she condescended to let him take the ghost of his dead mother, Semele, back to earth.

She was faithful to HADES, with whom she spent the four months of the earth's winter, apart from her love for ADONIS, who had been placed in her care by APHRODITE. You will recall that it was the magic girdle of APHRODITE that would deprive PERSEPHONE of her share of ADONIS' love.

When she held in her hand the pomegranate, it was to symbolise death and resurrection. Both PERSEPHONE and her companion, HECATE, represented the ancient hope of regeneration.

The black poplar was her tree, which grew in the Grove of PERSEPHONE, through which souls passed on their way to the palace of HADES.

HECATE

HECATE was the Goddess of Ghosts and Magic. She was the daughter of the Titan, PERSES, and the Titaness, ASTERIA. She was the companion of PERSEPHONE and it was her association with sorcery and black magic which probably led her to the lower world.

Accompanied by hell hounds, she was often depicted in triple form, looking down three roads at once. Could these roads have been those that led to Tartarus, Elysium and the Asphodel fields? Her three headed statue was to be found at many cross roads and on the eve of the full moon, offerings, normally of dog's flesh, were placed beneath her image. ZEUS gave to HECATE the power to bestow or withhold from mortals, any desired gift.

THANATOS

Son of NIGHT, brother of SLEEP, THANATOS was the God of Death. This dark robed master of the dead, carrying the inevitable sword, was known as the messenger of HADES.

Rarely thwarted in his grim errands, he was to lose a tremendous physical battle with HERACLES, over the rescue of Alcestis.

HYPNOS

HYPNOS was the God of Sleep, son of NIGHT and brother of DEATH. He lived in the underworld and never saw the sun, emerging only at night. Hesiod tell us that 'he comes softly and is sweet for men.'

Depicted as a young man with wings, he carried a branch in one hand with which he touched the foreheads of the tired. In the other hand was a horn, from which he poured a liquid that brought sleep.

Endymion, the most beautiful of men, was to be put to sleep by HYPNOS, but with open eyes.

HYPNOS had three sons who were the heralds of Dreams.

They were:

MORPHEUS, who came to the sleeper in human form.

IKELOS, who appeared in dreams as a beast, and PHANTASOS, who became all manner of inanimate objects to the dreamer.

THE ERINYES

The ERINYES were called FURIES by the Romans. They were the Guardians of Oaths, the winged deities of the underworld and servants of HADES.
These three daughters, who sprang from the spilt blood of URANUS, were known as:
ALECTO, whose will could not be opposed,
TISIPHONE, who avenged any murderous act, and
MEGAIRA, who was the personification of hatred.
Dressed in long, dark robes, their business was to punish the wicked.

A FURY

THE KERES

The KERES executed the will of the MOIRAE or FATES.
When the MOIRAE had settled the appointed hour of a person's life span, it was the KERES who came with DEATH to wield the final blow and conduct the deceased to the Kingdom of Shadows. They were often to be seen hovering like vultures on battle fields, or anywhere that death was imminent.

At the moment of death, the red robed KERES would cry hideously sinking their teeth into the victim and feeding on its blood.

They were the Dogs of HADES.

A HARPY

THE HARPIES

These were the two envoys of HADES, underworld deities known as the snatchers. They were the winged daughters of THAUMUS and ELECTRA, sisters of IRIS, the Goddess of the rainbow. They were called:

AELLOPUS, whose name meant 'storm wind', and OCYPETE, known as 'swift flying'.
Their task was to snatch the souls of the dead, a service they carried out with relish, for their master, HADES.

This brings to a close our Guide to the Greek Gods. We hope you have enjoyed reading about these 'larger than life' characters! You will meet many of them again when we return to bring you the tales of the Heroes, who had wonderful and terrible adventures, often thwarted by or assisted by the Gods, according to their desires or whims and in all sorts of disguises. We look forward to relating these daring exploits.